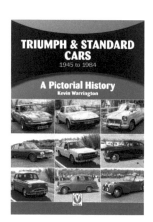

TRIUMPH & STANDARD
CARS
1945 to 1984

A Pictorial History
Kevin Warrington

T0386708

More from Veloce

www.veloce.co.uk

First published in April 2018, reprinted July 2022 by Veloce Publishing Limited, Veloce House, Parkway Farm Business Park, Middle Farm Way, Poundbury, Dorchester DT1 3AR, England.
Tel +44 (0)1305 260068 / Fax 01305 250479 / e-mail info@veloce.co.uk / web www.veloce.co.uk or www.velocebooks.com
ISBN: 978-1-787110-77-9 UPC: 6-36847-01077-5.

TRIUMPH & STANDARD CARS
1945 to 1984

A Pictorial History
Kevin Warrington

VELOCE

CONTENTS

ACKNOWLEDGEMENTS

For a relatively small company, Standard-Triumph created a large range of models between 1945 and 1984, and covering the entire range within a single volume has been an interesting task. It would not have been possible to provide such a comprehensive selection of photographs without the support of my friends Clive Wilkin and Colin Radford who provided me with some of their collection to choose from. Special thanks must be given to David Rowe, author of other titles in this *Pictorial History* series, who provided me with a huge selection of photographs covering some of the Standard models – Phase II Vanguards and 8s, 10s, and Pennants in particular, where I was lacking pictures and struggling to find suitable cars to photograph.

For the most part, technical information has been obtained from dealers' brochures and confirmed with data published as part of road tests in the many motoring magazines. The archives of the National Motor Museum at Beaulieu and the British Motor Museum at Gaydon have been most useful in this respect, and their staff, as always, more than willing to put up with the demands of a writer searching to confirm the most esoteric detail. I've also consulted the many books written by eminent author and motoring historian Graham Robson to verify where my memory has been lacking.

Detailing the colour schemes on offer proved to be more than a little difficult, with changes occurring frequently, especially during the 1970s. In this case, I have relied on the sales brochures to validate what the marketing department thought that the factory would be building, which I fully accept did not always totally correspond with what the customer could actually order, or what would be delivered.

Finally, I must thank all the staff at Veloce for their ongoing help and encouragement, the many Standard and Triumph owners' clubs whose resources and members have been unfailing with their assistance, and especially, my wife, Ann, for her help in proofreading and indulging my need to disappear to produce yet more photographs of classic cars.

Kevin Warrington

CHAPTER 1

WHERE IT ALL BEGAN

Standard and Triumph were entirely separate companies until 1945, both having their centre of operations in the Warwickshire town of Coventry, and neither able to claim to be amongst the 'big four' of British motor manufacturers. Whereas Standard had built its reputation on constructing worthy and dependable motor cars and setting 'The Standard' for the industry to follow, Triumph's products had a more sporting and flamboyant air to them from the earliest days. The Standard Motor Company, as well as building complete vehicles sold under its own brand, had established a worthwhile business as a supplier of major components, including engines and transmissions to smaller niche players such as SS Cars and Morgan.

Dating from 1929, this fabric-bodied Standard 9 Teignmouth had a 1287cc side valve engine and three-speed transmission. It was amongst the last models to be fitted with the traditional shouldered Standard radiator.

Triumph's offering in the 7hp and 8hp class was the 'Super Seven,' the side valve engine of which displaced 832cc, and was available in numerous body styles. This survivor is a simple two-door saloon.

Triumph had begun as a manufacturing company building pedal cycles. Installing an internal combustion engine into a pedal cycle frame created an early motorcycle, and a contract to supply the Army during the 1914-18 conflict provided a worthwhile business opportunity, leading ultimately to the first Triumph car. Finances were always difficult, and a series of disposals resulted in Triumph selling off its interests in pedal cycles in 1932 and the motorcycle business in 1936. The end came to the Triumph company in 1939 when the Bank called in the liquidators, and the remains of the business were sold on to Thomas W Ward & Co.

When peace came in 1945, little survived of Triumph and it was again put up for sale. In reality, all that was for sale was the name and the collateral value of the brand; nearly all the physical assets of the business had been destroyed, and it was the Standard Motor Company that came to the rescue.

Standard had been established in 1903 by Reginald Maudslay, a trained civil engineer and cousin of Cyril Maudslay, founder of the commercial vehicle company that bore the family name. Clearly unable to use the name for his own car business, Reginald Maudslay settled on the name 'Standard' – a word

then conveying its dictionary meaning, and emphasising the measure of quality to which other manufacturers might aspire, rather than its more modern connotations as 'regular' or 'typical.'

In 1930, one of the great names of the British motor industry, Captain (later Sir) John Black joined 'the Standard' from Hillman, becoming Managing Director. Under Black's management the company was to thrive, although his management style has frequently been described as 'mercurial' and 'abrasive.' Having previously been rebuffed in attempts to acquire the business of both Morgan and SS Cars (soon to be renamed as Jaguar), the opportunity for Standard to acquire Triumph in 1945 was enthusiastically grabbed, as was an arrangement to build tractors for Ferguson, providing increased profits and thus funding for new models. This latter arrangement also made good use of a former wartime shadow factory that had been acquired at an advantageous price by Standard, following its wartime contribution, building, amongst other things, Mosquito aircraft.

Triumph cars adopted Art Deco styling in the 1930s, especially for the radiator grille, which was not to everyone's taste. This Dolomite 2-litre, a model name that will reappear much later, boasted an overhead valve six-cylinder engine of 1991cc, placing it in the 16hp taxation bracket, and four-speed synchromesh transmission.

Standard's cars of the same era were a little more refined in design; this one is a Flying 12 dating from 1938 with a 1608cc side valve engine.

Thus, it was in 1945 that the company became known as Standard-Triumph International Ltd. Both brand names would continue to be used with the Triumph name given to the products with more overtly sporting characteristics until 1963, whenceforth all models were sold under the Triumph brand.

Financial difficulties were never far away, and the late 1950s saw a time of difficulty once again, with a product range desperate for investment and little cash to fund it. Salvation came in 1960, when truck and bus manufacturer Leyland Motors, keen to re-establish a presence in passenger car manufacturing, purchased Standard-Triumph for £20 million. This provided the investment funding for a product-led revival, assisted by a close association with Italian maestro stylist Giovanni Michelotti providing a recognisable style to most future products that would emerge from the Canley works. A major reorganisation of the national motor industry in 1968, encouraged by the government of the time, saw Leyland Motors merge with British Motor Holdings, the latter being the result of a previous merger between BMC and Jaguar, to form British Leyland Motor Corporation. With BLMC eventually taken into public ownership, the Triumph name was last seen on a car of Japanese origin, assembled at the former Morris Motors premises at Cowley near Oxford. This final venture was to provide a blueprint for future co-operation with Honda, until that, too, came to an end, with the purchase of the remains of the former British Leyland business by BMW. Inevitably, the business was again to be sold on.

To end this short historical overview on a positive note, amongst all the brand names that were acquired, BMW has retained the 'Triumph' marque, and perhaps, one day, we may again see the name displayed on a new motor car.

CHAPTER 2

EARLY POSTWAR CARS

With the coming of peace in 1945 and the acquisition of Triumph by the Standard Motor Company, the first models to be put on the market were the Standard cars that had been the mainstay of the company when production had ceased in 1939 at the outbreak of the Second World War. There were to be minor differences in the new models, the most distinctive of which was to be the deletion of the slats from the bonnet sides.

8HP, 12HP and 14HP

Three model types were built: 8HP in saloon, tourer and drophead coupé form, all powered by a four-cylinder side valve engine of 1009cc. Postwar cars were also provided with a four-speed gearbox. Similarly, the Standard 12HP and 14HP cars were

In common with almost every other motor manufacturer, Standard-Triumph's immediate postwar cars were a continuation of late 1930s production with just minor changes. In the case of the Standard 8 seen here, the most obvious point of recognition is the plain sided bonnet, compared with the prewar model which was equipped with horizontal cooling slats. Although the general appearance of cars from all the large manufacturers were visually very similar at this time, the Standard was better specified than, for example, the Ford Anglia.

Dating from 1947, this drophead coupé Standard 8 illustrates the alternative style that was offered. Like the saloon, the plain bonnet confirms this as a postwar vehicle.

By modern standards, the instrument panel of this 8 is simple, but for its period was comprehensively equipped with an ammeter, oil pressure gauge and fuel gauge. Dual wipers were fitted to the opening windscreen and the 'umbrella' style handbrake can be seen. The steering wheel lock, hazard light switch and cigarette lighter power socket are all modern additions.

The Triumph Roadster, despite being a completely new car for 1946 could easily be thought of as a 1930s throwback; its style remaining like the Dolomite roadster of ten years earlier. The front bumper-mounted turn indicators of this car are a modern addition in the interest of road safety, with the original semaphore 'trafficator' being just visible behind the B post hinged 'suicide' door. An unusual feature of the Roadster was the wide, shallow windscreen requiring the fitting of three wipers to clear it.

reintroduced, fitted with 1609cc and 1766cc side valve four-cylinder engines.

COLOURS: Black, Grey
ENGINE:
8HP – 1009cc, four-cylinder, side valve, bore 56.7mm, stroke 100mm, power 28bhp.
12HP – 1609cc, four-cylinder, side valve, bore 69.5mm, stroke 106mm, power 44bhp.
14HP – 1776cc, four-cylinder, side valve, bore 73mm, stroke 106mm, power 65bhp.
GEARBOX: Four-speed with synchromesh on top three speeds, floor change.
Overall gearing ratios:
8HP – 1st 20.29:1, 2nd 12.48, 3rd 7.46, top 5.14, reverse 20.29.
12HP – 1st 19.8, 2nd 11.8, 3rd 7.06, top 4.86, reverse 19.8.
14HP – 1st 18.04, 2nd 11.1, 3rd 6.64, top 4.57, reverse 18.04.
REAR AXLE: Semi-floating. Ratio: 5.14:1 (8HP), 4.86:1 (12HP), 4.57:1 (14HP).
BRAKES: Mechanically operated on all models using Bendix enclosed cables operating drums all round.
SUSPENSION: Front: independent with transverse leaf spring and wishbones; rear live axle and semi-elliptic springs. Lever arm dampers.
STEERING: 8HP – Burman-Douglas worm and nut; **12HP/14HP** – Marles cam and twin roller.
DIMENSIONS:
8HP – length 139in (3530mm), width 56in (1422mm).

Wet weather equipment consisted of a close-fitting folding roof and wind-up windows in the doors. Rear 'dickey seat' passengers were protected by the fold out windscreen, but were otherwise exposed to the elements.

12HP & 14HP – length 165in (4191mm), width 59in (1498mm).
FUEL CAPACITY: 8HP – 6 gallons (27 litres), 12/14HP – 8 gallons (36.5 litres).
PERFORMANCE: The manufacturer's quoted top speed for all three cars was respectable for a family car of the period, with the 14HP car achieving 70mph and a 0 to 50mph time of 22 seconds; the 12HP was a little slower at 65mph in 26 seconds, while the 8HP was still capable of a reasonable 60mph, although it would take 30 seconds to achieve 50mph.

The first all new models: 18TR and 20TR Roadster

New models were announced in March 1946 – the new Roadster, described below, and the 'Town and Country Saloon,' later to evolve into the Renown, described in the next chapter. The Roadster set no new standards for design; in many respects it was a continuation of the prewar Triumph styling, but gained a reputation for being the last car design to incorporate a 'dickey seat,' allegedly a feature much liked by Sir John Black, despite being an anachronism.

Chassis design was of tubular steel section, hand welded, with a transverse spring providing independent front suspension and semi-elliptic springs at the rear supporting a live axle. From 1946 to 1948, power came from a revised prewar engine of 1776cc capacity, now fitted with overhead valve gear replacing the earlier side valve, delivered through a four-speed gearbox operated by a column gear change situated on the right-hand side of the steering column. Models were designated 18TR.

Between 1948 and 1950, the car was fitted with a new four-cylinder engine of 2088cc, and a three-speed transmission, still column change operated, but fitted to the left side, and these cars had the model designation of 20TR. This engine would form the backbone of Standard-Triumph production throughout the 1950s and 60s, not ending production until the introduction of the TR5 in 1967.

The coachwork, designed by Frank Callaby and Arthur Ballard was conventionally built on traditional ash

Again, the amber turn signals are a modern addition to the rear wings. Here, the rear 'dickey seat' is shown in the open position; passengers would gain access using the rubber treads on the rear bumper, and were provided with their own windscreen which, when folded, would form part of the luggage compartment cover. Casual observers, not being fully familiar with the features of this car, may be confused to notice that the luggage compartment had been fitted with windows, but when the dickey seat was not required, the car offered a large boot.

Clearly visible are the deeply recessed radiator, the large headlamps, dual horns and additional lamps, all finished in chrome, presenting a bright, shining image in the grey and austere postwar years.

frames covered in aluminium panels. These panels were produced on rubber presses that had manufactured aluminium panels for the de Havilland Mosquito aircraft, built during hostilities at the 'shadow factory' operated by the Standard Motor Company on behalf of the Ministry of Aircraft Production.

Looking into the passenger compartment of this Roadster, the wide seat, large steering wheel and column change are clear to see. The right-hand gear change confirms this as an 18TR model.

Boot space on the Roadster was reasonable, provided that additional passengers were not being carried. The occasional seats are shown here folded.

The Roadster gained much fame during the 1980s when it featured in the BBC TV series *Bergerac*, starring actor John Nettles.

COLOURS: Black, Dark Metallic Grey, Maroon.

ENGINE:
18TR models – 1776cc, four-cylinder, overhead valve, bore 73mm, stroke 106mm, power 65bhp.
20TR models – 2088cc, four-cylinder , overhead valve, bore 85mm, stroke 92mm, power 68bhp.
GEARBOX:
18TR – Four-speed with synchromesh on top three speeds, column change.
Overall gearing ratios: 1st 18.04:1, 2nd 11.1:1, 3rd 6.64:1, top 4.57:1, reverse 18.04:1.
20TR – Three-speed with synchromesh on all speeds, column change.
Overall gearing ratios: 1st 16.73:1, 2nd 7.71:1, top 4.625:1, reverse 18.99:1.
REAR AXLE: Semi-floating. Ratio 4.56:1 (18TR) or 4.625:1 (20TR).
BRAKES: Girling 'Hydrastatic,' operating 10in x 1.5in drums all round.
SUSPENSION: Front: independent with transverse leaf spring and wishbones; rear live axle and semi-elliptic springs. Lever arm dampers.
STEERING: Marles cam and twin roller.
DIMENSIONS: Length: 168.5in (4280mm), width 64in (1625mm).
FUEL CAPACITY: 10 gallons (45 litres)
PRODUCTION: approximately 2500 18TR models and 2000 20TR models
PERFORMANCE: Standard Triumph quoted a maximum speed of 84mph for the 1776cc model in original sales literature for the car. A road test published in *Autocar* gave a top speed of 75mph, and 0-60mph figure of 34.4 seconds, and a later test with the 2088cc-engined car resulted in performance of 77mph, but with a much improved 0-60mph time of 27.9 seconds.

CHAPTER 3

THE 'RAZOR EDGE' TRIUMPHS

Coach-built cars and limousines of the 1930s had adopted a style with very sharp edges that had become known popularly as 'razor edge.' When mounted on the mechanicals of Rolls-Royce and Bentley, the overall impression was one of elegance and style, and, by repute, appealed to Sir John Black, who determined that this form of styling should have a place in the planned four-door car, of about two litres, that would complement the Roadster described earlier. Generically now commonly known as 'Renowns,' the four-door cars spanned a series of different models, and a similar style motif was also to be used on a smaller, two-door car sold as the Triumph Mayflower, where, perhaps, the design did not work quite so well.

The side profile shows off the elegant proportions of the car that reflects the 'razor edge' design. Lever door handles signify that this is an early car, believed to be an 1800 'Town and Country' model. In common with many 1950s and earlier cars, flashing amber turn signals have been fitted to the rear wings to replace the B pillar mounted semaphore trafficators.

1800 – Town and Country Saloon 18TD

The first model to appear in 1946, along with the Roadster, was the Triumph 1800 'Town and Country Saloon,' built on a modified Standard 12 mechanical platform. The body design was created by Standard-Triumph stylist Walter Belgrove after an initial design by coachbuilder Mulliners was rejected. The bodywork was, however, built by Mulliner at its Birmingham plant and shipped to Standard-Triumph for assembly. Utilising a chassis again built from tubular steel because of shortages of steel plate for pressing, the body was constructed mostly of aluminium panels over an ash frame, and was mechanically similar to the 18TR Roadster. The model had the designation of 18TD.

COLOURS: Black, Dark Metallic Grey, Maroon.
ENGINE: 1776cc, four-cylinder, overhead valve, bore 73mm, stroke 106mm, power 65bhp.
GEARBOX: Four-speed with synchromesh on top three speeds, column change. Overall gearing ratios: 1st 19.18:1, 2nd 11.8:1, 3rd 7.06:1, top 4.86:1, reverse 19.18:1.
REAR AXLE: Semi-floating. Ratio 4.86:1.

BRAKES: Girling 'Hydrastatic,' operating 10in x 1.5in drums all round.
SUSPENSION: Front: independent with transverse leaf spring and wishbones; rear: live axle and semi-elliptic springs. Lever arm dampers.
STEERING: Marles cam and twin roller.
DIMENSIONS: Length: 176in (4470mm), width 64in (1625mm).
FUEL CAPACITY: 10 gallons (45 litres).
PRODUCTION: Approximately 1000.
PERFORMANCE: Standard Triumph quoted a maximum speed of 80mph in the original sales literature for the car and a 0 to 50mph 'through the gears' time of 16 seconds.

Town and Country Saloon TDA

In 1949, in common with the Roadster, the 2088cc engine and three-speed gearbox was fitted, creating the model designation TDA. This model had a short life and production run of 2000 examples.

COLOURS: Black, Dark Metallic Grey, Maroon.
ENGINE: 2088cc, four-cylinder, overhead valve, bore 85mm, stroke 92mm, power 68bhp.
GEARBOX: Three-speed with synchromesh on all speeds, column change.

Overall gearing ratios: 1st 16.73:1, 2nd 7.71:1, top 4.625:1, reverse 18.99:1.
REAR AXLE: Semi-floating. Ratio 4.625:1.
BRAKES: Girling 'Hydrastatic,' operating 10in x 1.5in drums all round.
SUSPENSION: Front: independent with transverse leaf spring and wishbones; rear live axle and semi-elliptic springs. Lever arm dampers.
STEERING: Marles cam and twin roller.
DIMENSIONS: Length: 176in (4470mm), width 64in (1625mm).
FUEL CAPACITY: 10 gallons (45 litres).
PRODUCTION: 2000 TDA models.

Renown TDB

Later in 1949 substantial changes were made, taking advantage of the availability of steel plate to allow a more modern box section steel chassis to be utilised, in common with the recently introduced Standard Vanguard. The 2088cc engine and three-speed column change transmission

were retained, but significant enhancements were made to the front suspension, now based on coil springs and wishbones rather than the transverse leaf spring of earlier iterations. Inside, the instruments were changed to now be the same as those fitted in the Vanguard, but, in keeping with the 'leather and walnut' style of the car, the instruments were fitted into a wooden dashboard. With these changes, a new name was announced – the Triumph Renown – and given the designation TDB.

COLOURS: Black, Dark Metallic Grey, Maroon, Jade Green.
ENGINE: 2088cc, four-cylinder, overhead valve, bore 85mm, stroke 92mm, power 68bhp.
GEARBOX: Three-speed with synchromesh on all speeds, column change. Optional overdrive working on top gear available from 1950. Overall gearing ratios: 1st 16.73:1, 2nd 7.71:1, top 4.625:1, reverse 18.99:1. Overdrive ratio 1:1.18, later revised to 1:1.28.
REAR AXLE: Semi-floating. Ratio 4.625:1.

The mascot fitted to the radiator filler cap and simple door handles identify this car as a Renown TDB. The 'torch' mascot was fitted approximately midway through the TDB production. Later in the production of the TDB model, the rising cost of chrome plating resulted in the headlamp shells being finished in body colour paint, although chrome plating was to return later during the production run of the TDC model.

BRAKES: Hydraulic operating 9in x 1.75in drums all round.
SUSPENSION: Front: independent with coil springs and wishbones; rear: live axle and semi-elliptic springs. Lever arm dampers.
STEERING: Marles cam and twin roller.
DIMENSIONS: Length: 176in (4470mm), width 64in (1625mm).
FUEL CAPACITY: 14 gallons (63.5 litres).
PRODUCTION: 6501 TDB models.

Renown TDC and Limousine

A further model change came in 1951 with the introduction of a modestly stretched limousine version of the Renown, complete with glazed partition between the driver and rear passenger compartment. Normally, when manufacturers create a limousine version from an existing car, the additional length is inserted from the B post rearwards, but in the case of the Renown, it was spread equally between front and rear compartments. Occasional rear seats, another common feature of a limousine, were not included, and, with the driver's seat being fixed in position, the appeal of the car was very limited, resulting in overall sales of less than 200 cars. However, the new lengthened bodyshell and extended chassis were introduced in 1952 as a mark two version of the Renown, designated as a TDC, and would continue until production finally ended in October 1954. Specifications for limousine and TDC models as TDB, except as follows:

DIMENSIONS: Length: 181in (4597mm), width 64in (1625mm).
PRODUCTION: 189 limousines, 2800 TDC models.

A close up of the front of this 1800 'Town and Country' shows the expanse of chrome plate and large headlamps giving a visually similar appearance to the contemporary Triumph Roadster. Again, the amber turn signals are a much later addition.

In a world of rather drab black and grey cars, the maroon finish of this model would brighten up an early 1950s day.

Looking as good as the day they left the factory, these two Renown TDCs show the extra body length and push-button door handles. A roof mounted aerial for the, presumably valve, wireless gives an air of quality.

Above the waistline, the similarity of the Mayflower to the larger Renown is clear to see.

The slab-sided appearance is very clear in this view. The amber turn signals are a later addition.

Mayflower

The Triumph Mayflower was introduced to the car-buying public at the London Motor Show in September 1949, with first sales starting shortly thereafter. The idea behind the model was to produce a small car that would sell well in export markets, particularly the USA, which could well have influenced its name. The 'razor edge' styling, at least from the waist upwards, shared some similarity with the larger Renown models, and the rear profile was visually similar, but, viewed from the side, the two cars shared little else. Built as a two-door, four-seat car, it was aimed at an entirely different market, and perhaps the most complimentary thing said about the model was a remark about it being a 'charm bracelet Rolls-Royce.' It was, however, the first Standard-Triumph to be built as a monocoque, and the general arrangement of the front suspension would find uses in future models. Power came from an engine with its origins in the prewar Standard 10, complete with side valves but now fitted with a new aluminium alloy cylinder head, and was transmitted through a three-speed

Mayflowers were supplied from the factory in a limited number of colours, with most being finished in either grey or black. This example is finished in maroon: a colour also available on the larger Renown.

gearbox operated by a column change. A drophead model also joined the range, but only ten were built. Mayflower production ceased in 1953.

Mayflowers were also built in Australia, where a wider range of colours were available and, uniquely, a pick-up version ('ute' in local vernacular) was available.

COLOURS: Black, Dark Metallic Grey, Maroon, Jade Green.
ENGINE: 1247cc, four-cylinder, side valve, bore 63mm, stroke 100mm, power 38bhp.
GEARBOX: Three-speed with synchromesh on all speeds, column change. Overall gearing ratios: 1st 18.14:1, 2nd 8.56:1, top 5.125:1, reverse 21.04:1.
REAR AXLE: Semi-floating. Ratio 5.125:1.
BRAKES: Hydraulic operating 8in x 1.5in drums all round.
SUSPENSION: Front: independent with coil springs and wishbones; rear: live axle and semi-elliptic springs. Telescopic dampers.
STEERING: Cam and lever.
DIMENSIONS: Length: 154in (3912mm), width 62in (1575mm).
FUEL CAPACITY: 10 gallons (45 litres).
PERFORMANCE: Top speed 65mph; 0-60mph in 27 seconds.
PRODUCTION: 35,000 models.

The dashboard styling for the Mayflower was simple and plain, providing just the essentials of speedometer, ammeter fuel and temperature gauges. The left-hand column gear change is also visible.

An early Phase I Vanguard finished in attractive gold colour, which must have looked quite remarkable in the drab austerity times of the late 1940s. The radiator grille was only used on the Phase I cars, and the lack of separate sidelights show this to be an early model.

Another very early example: this one shows the long doors and hidden sills to good effect.

CHAPTER 4

THE STANDARD VANGUARD FAMILY

Highly influenced by US designs, especially those of the contemporary Plymouth, Standard launched their new Vanguard model in 1947. It was a model that was to go through various iterations until its final demise in 1963, when it would be the final car to bear the name 'Standard.' Use of language changes with time, and what once was a name that gave the impression of a brand to emulate and look up to had become a word that implied basic. Stories abound of potential customers who viewed the cars and enquired whether perhaps a 'deluxe' version was available.

Vanguard Phase I

The early Phase I 'beetle back' six-light car was heavily influenced by American styling, following the desires of Sir John Black, who had dispatched Chief Stylist Walter Belgrove to Grosvenor Square in London to study and sketch the current styling of US cars outside the US Embassy. A very robust, comfortable and spacious car was the result, and it was to sell strongly in export markets, especially

Separate sidelights were added from mid-1949.

in the developing British Commonwealth countries.

The very earliest cars can be identified by doors that overlap the sills, an ornate radiator grille, sidelight integrated into the main headlights and a small rear window. The gear change was also positioned on the outer side of the steering wheel. Separate sidelights were added in the early part of 1949.

The doors were soon modified to finish above the sills to provide greater clearance against high kerbs, this change occurring during 1949, when a bonnet mascot was also added, and the gear change lever moved to the opposite side of the steering column, towards the centre of the car. Removable spats now partially covered the rear wheels.

Later modifications, creating the 'Phase IA' model, followed for 1952, and can be identified by a larger rear window, a less ornate radiator grille and, more subtly, a lower bonnet line. The door handles were now of the push button style, and the dishes beneath the handles in the door skin pressings were removed. The company's sales literature for 1952 lists leather seats and a push button radio set as options, along with the unusual option, at least for UK market cars, of air-conditioning.

Rear view of early Vanguard showing small rear window and simple rear light fittings. The chrome exhaust pipe is a more recent addition.

A comprehensive set of instruments was fitted to the Vanguard: speedometer, fuel, temperature and oil pressure gauges and ammeter. The heater controls can be seen close to the steering column and the left hand gear change is also visible.

Revisions to the front grille provide an easy point of identification for a Phase IA model Vanguard as seen in this image.

Revisions to the rear of the car created a larger rear window for the Phase IA, and relocation of the rear number plate.

An example of a rare Vanguard estate car.

In addition to the saloon, an estate car was available, as were commercial variations (see later in this book for details of the commercial models). A small number of convertibles were built and sold in Belgium by Imperia, a company with an agreement to assemble Standard cars.

COLOURS: As well as the usual grey and black, the Vanguard was available finished in silver, gold or green metallic.
ENGINE: 2088cc, four-cylinder, overhead valve, bore 85mm, stroke 92mm, power 68bhp.
GEARBOX: Three-speed with synchromesh on all speeds, column change.
Overall gearing ratios: 1st 16.73:1, 2nd 7.71:1, top 4.625:1, reverse 18.99:1. Overdrive ratio 1:1.18, later revised to 1:1.28.

REAR AXLE: Semi-floating. Ratio 4.625:1.
BRAKES: Hydraulic operating 9in x 1.75in drums all round.
SUSPENSION: Front: independent with coil springs and wishbones; rear live axle and semi-elliptic springs. Lever arm dampers and anti-roll bar.
STEERING: Cam and twin roller.
DIMENSIONS: Length: 166in (4216mm), width 69in (1753mm). Estate car 163in (4140mm).
FUEL CAPACITY: 15 gallons (68 litres).
PRODUCTION: In total, just short of 175,000 Phase I and IA models were produced.
PERFORMANCE: The sales literature claims a maximum speed of 80mph and 16 seconds to achieve a speed of 50mph while returning 24-26 miles per imperial gallon.

Vanguard Phase II

Following the 'Phase IA' models, more drastic changes immediately followed to produce, logically, the 'Phase II.' Mechanically similar to the earlier design, except that the clutch was now hydraulically operated, and the body was now of what was to become known as a 'three box' or 'ponton' style. From a practical viewpoint, this provided more usable boot space with greater headroom for rear seat passengers and wider doors providing easier access. During 1954, Standard-Triumph announced diesel power as an option – a first for any UK manufactured passenger car. Installation of the heavier, oil burning motor required strengthening of the chassis, and starting the engine from cold was an involved process requiring the use of an excess fuelling device and decompressing the engine.

The visual appearance at the front of the car was little changed with the introduction of the Phase II models. The large rear window and reshaped doors can be clearly seen while at the front, the radiator grille has been simplified, and additional chrome trim fills the gap between the grille and the sidelights.

COLOURS: Additional, brighter colours especially blues and greens were now available in addition to the traditional black or grey.
ENGINE: Petrol: 2088cc, four-cylinder, overhead valve, bore 85mm, stroke 92mm, power 68bhp. **Diesel:** 2092cc, four-cylinder, overhead valve, bore 81mm, stroke 101.6mm, power 40bhp.
GEARBOX: Three-speed with synchromesh on all speeds, column change. Overall gearing ratios: 1st 16.73:1, 2nd 7.71:1, top 4.625:1, reverse 18.99:1. Overdrive ratio 1:1.28, operating on 2nd and top, giving, effectively, five speeds.
REAR AXLE: Semi-floating. Ratio 4.625:1.
BRAKES: Hydraulic operating 9in x 1.75in drums all round.
SUSPENSION: Front: independent with coil springs and wishbones; rear live axle and semi-elliptic springs. Lever arm dampers.
STEERING: Cam and twin roller.
DIMENSIONS: Length: 168in (4267mm), width 69in (1753mm). Estate car 163in (4140mm).
FUEL CAPACITY: 12 gallons (54.5 litres).
PRODUCTION: 81,074 Phase II Vanguards were produced, of which less than 2000 were fitted with the diesel engine.
PERFORMANCE: Performance of the petrol-

A rear three-quarter view shows substantial modifications on the Phase II. The 'ponton' styling bears a resemblance to the Rover P4 and Mercedes-Benz saloons of the same era.

engined car remained similar to the earlier model. *Motor* magazine road tested a diesel-engined Vanguard in 1954, and recorded a top speed of 66.2mph and a leisurely through the gears acceleration time of 31.6 seconds to achieve 50mph.

Vanguard Phase III, Vignale, Ensign & Sportsman

The final Vanguard, the Phase III, was announced in 1955 with a completely new body style, and now featuring unitary construction. To maintain market confidence, which had some concerns regarding the economics of repairing lightly crash-damaged monocoque bodies, the wings were fitted to the body structure by bolts to allow for easier replacement. A single-piece curved windscreen replaced the

The final 'Phase' in the Vanguard story was a complete break from earlier designs, showing a strong transatlantic influence.

Duotone finish for the Vanguard was a popular option.

now old-fashioned split screen style used in the earlier cars. Overall, the new car was longer and lower, but slightly narrower than the outgoing model, and the elimination of a separate chassis allowed for a reduction of some 200lb (89kg) in the overall weight of the car. Despite the all new appearance, most of the mechanical underpinnings were carried over from the earlier models, but the option of diesel power was quietly deleted. Revised overall gearing resulted in similar levels of performance with improved fuel economy.

Styling of the new model was trusted to an American industrial designer, Carl Otto, who had experience with the famous US designer Raymond Loewry, and manufacture of the bodyshell was contracted to Pressed Steel. The style was to have the longest life of all the Vanguard variants, finally ending production in 1963. Cars were built as four-door saloons, estate cars, and in Australia as a pickup, known locally as a 'ute.'

A series of detail changes took place prior to the end of production, all using the same basic body shape and mechanicals. First to market was the Vanguard Phase III, which was built between October 1955 and October 1957, with a deluxe version built between November 1956 and September 1958. With the car now being three years old, a midlife 'face-lift' project was entrusted to Italian coachbuilder Vignale, and a rising designer who would go on to a long relationship with Standard-Triumph: Giovanni Michelotti.

The changes provided increased glass area to the front and rear windscreens, and a revised grille. These revised cars were badged as Vanguard Vignale, first built in October 1958, and continuing until August 1961. The range of colour finishes increased, including a number of dual colour combinations which suited the style well. With the Vignale came the option of a four-speed gearbox with floor change, or traditional three-speed column change, both with the option of overdrive. An automatic gearbox was also listed. At the end of the Vanguard's life and pre-dating its use in the replacement Triumph 2000 model, a new six-cylinder engine of nominal two litre

Fitted with a large chrome grille, early intentions of launching the Vanguard Sportsman under the Triumph brand are clear.

capacity was fitted to create the Standard Vanguard Vignale Six.

A more basic model, fitted with a smaller capacity engine and marketed as the Standard Ensign, was built between October 1957 and May 1963, and found great favour with large fleet buyers, especially the Armed Forces. Latterly, a deluxe version of this car was announced, as was a further revision of the engine at the end of production with the same capacity as the Triumph TR4. All the above models were available as either saloon or estate cars. The estate cars featured a split tailgate that allowed extra long loads to be carried.

A final variation on the theme was built in small numbers between 1956 and 1958 and intended as a model to continue the Triumph Renown name to continue after the razor edge bodied car had ended production. This car was powered by an engine that shared characteristics with the Triumph TR3, and was fitted with a large chromed radiator grille bearing a Triumph globe emblem. Ultimately, the Triumph name was not used, and the car came to market as the Vanguard Sportsman. It was not to be a commercial success, but could be purchased to special order until 1960.

COLOURS: Coffee, Pale Yellow, Phantom Grey, Cotswold Blue, Litchfield Green. When a duotone finish was specified, these colours would be used on the roof and lower body with a choice of the following for the upper body: Pink Wisteria, Nimbus White, Powder Blue.

A Vanguard Vignale is followed into the arena by an Ensign. The duotone paint finish was introduced with the Vignale, as were larger windscreens front and rear, a revised grille and additional chrome.

Viewed from the rear, the enlarged rear screen and revised lighting clusters of this Vanguard Vignale can be seen. The rear foglamp is a modern addition.

This Vignale estate car has arrived at an event towing a caravan, an activity well suited to the car – the clue being the extension mirrors. The duotone colour finish suits this car well.

Ensigns were supplied with a simplified grille and lower specification of trim, in line with their reduced list price, which made them attractive to fleet users and the Armed Forces, which accumulated a substantial fleet. The door mirrors on this car are a much later addition.

ENGINE:

Vanguard III, Vanguard Vignale – Petrol: 2088cc, four-cylinder, overhead valve, bore 85mm, stroke 92mm, power 68bhp.
Vanguard Sportsman – Petrol: as Vanguard III, except fitted with twin SU carburettors, power 90bhp.
Vanguard Vignale Six – Petrol: 1998cc, six-cylinder, overhead valve, bore 74.7mm, stroke 76mm, power 85bhp.
Ensign – Petrol: 1670cc, four-cylinder, overhead valve, bore 76mm, stroke 92mm, power 60bhp.
Ensign Deluxe – Petrol: 2138cc, four-cylinder, overhead valve, bore 86mm, stroke 92mm, power 75bhp.

GEARBOX:

Three-speed with synchromesh on all speeds, column change. Overall gearing ratios: 1st 15.2:1, 2nd 7.17:1, top 4.3:1, reverse 17.7:1. **Sportsman:** 1st 16.1:1, 2nd 7.6:1, top 4.55:1, reverse 18.72:1. Overdrive ratio 1:1.28, operating on 2nd and top giving effectively five speeds.
Four-speed with synchromesh, floor change. Overall gearing ratios: 1st 15.2:1, 2nd 9.03:1, 3rd 5.96:1, top 4.3:1, reverse 19.6:1.
Vanguard Vignale Six and Ensign: 1st 14.5:1; 2nd 8.61:1; 3rd 5.66:1; top, 4.1:1, reverse 18.64:1. Overdrive ratio 1:1.28, operating on 3rd and top giving effectively six speeds.

A Borg-Warner three-speed epicyclic automatic gearbox coupled with a torque converter was available as an option.

Although the Ensign was not offered as an estate model, the Ensign Deluxe was, as seen here. The full-length folding sunroof was not a factory option, and would have been fitted as an aftermarket accessory.

REAR AXLE: Semi-floating. Ratio 4.3:1 (4.55:1 for Sportsman and 4.1:1 for Ensign and Vignale Six).

BRAKES: Hydraulic operating 9in x 2.25in drums all round. 10in on Sportsman and later models. Front disc brakes listed as an option on Vignale Six.

SUSPENSION: Front: independent with coil springs and wishbones; rear: live axle and semi-elliptic springs. Lever arm dampers.

STEERING: Recirculating ball.

DIMENSIONS: Length: 172in (4368mm), width 67.5in (1714mm). Estate car 173.5in (4407mm).

FUEL CAPACITY: 12 gallons for saloon (54.5 litres), 14 gallons for estates (63.5 litres).

PRODUCTION: Vanguard III – 37,194; Sportsman – 901; **Ensign and Ensign deluxe** – 21,170; **Vanguard Vignale** – 26,276; Vanguard Six – 9953.

PERFORMANCE: A magazine article in the early 1960s reports a trip in a Vanguard Six where a top speed of 'over 90mph' was obtained with a comfortable cruising speed of 80mph. Similar figures are quoted elsewhere for the maximum speed of the Sportsman, with a 0-60mph time of 19.2 seconds, while the manufacturer's brochures claim a top speed of 84mph and through the gears acceleration of 20 seconds to 60mph for the Vanguard III and Vignale. Performance of the 1670cc-engined Ensign was less exciting with a test in *Motor* indicating a top speed of 77.6mph and 24.4 seconds to reach 60mph.

The Vanguard Six was also available as an estate car.

The driver's view of a Vanguard Six fitted with optional automatic transmission. The full complement of instruments is also fitted, as is a radio.

Sporting a popular period sunvisor, the Vanguard Six topped the range.

A very early, original specification Standard 8, showing the sliding windows and the absence of hubcaps.

Lacking an opening boot cover, access to the spare wheel is via the removable panel surrounding the number plate, and luggage is accessed via the rear doors and hinged rear seats.

A very basic set of instruments was fitted to both the 8 and 10, with just a speedometer and fuel gauge being specified.

CHAPTER 5
STANDARD'S NEW SMALL CAR – THE 8 AND 10

The replacement for the Triumph Mayflower came onto the market in 1953 as a rival for the Morris Minor and Austin A30, both of which were being produced by the newly formed British Motor Corporation at the time of the introduction of the new Standard.

Built of monocoque construction and with an entirely new engine, the trim of the early 8 was spartan in the extreme. To reduce the price as far as possible, but still return a profit, the specification was minimal, with sliding windows and, most notably, no opening lid to access the luggage compartment, which was instead accessed by folding the rear seats forward. Clever marketing saw this last feature sold as a benefit to the owner by increasing the security of the contents. Access to the spare wheel was by removal of a cover positioned below where one might have expected to find the boot lid.

The engine with the code name SC shared some similarity to the new A series from BMC, but was of entirely different design. It would serve Standard-Triumph and eventually British Leyland for many years, with its capacity and power output being increased to meet the requirements of newer models.

A deluxe model was introduced in 1954, introducing wind-up windows, but an opening boot lid would not be fitted until 1957. From 1955, the basic car was renamed the 'Family 8' and the deluxe became the Super. For those wanting more power, the Standard 10 also joined the model range in 1954, bringing a few more creature comforts and a new chromed frontal appearance. An unusual option available on the 10 was the Smiths semi-automatic system marketed as 'Standrive.' Uptake was poor and the system was problematic.

An estate car joined the model range in 1955, sold initially as the Standard 10 'Good Companion,' and latterly just as Companion. Commercial vehicle versions were also produced, and were very popular in their time, being simple, competitively priced, and workmanlike vehicles.

'Gold Star' versions with increased power versions and a higher compression ratio were followed in 1957 by a face-lifted model, which was marketed as the Standard Pennant. Longer front and rear wings followed the fashion trends of the time, with hooded headlamps and the impressions of fins to the rear. Internally, the trim was enhanced and a remote gear change was fitted. More chrome was added at the front to create a distinctive grille, and a chromed waist adornment allowed a range of two tone paint finishes to be produced.

A Standard Super 8 could be identified by the chrome 'moustache' over the radiator aperture, and a conventionally opening boot.

COLOURS: In the sales brochure published in October 1958, the following colours were offered: Phantom Grey, Pale Yellow, Powder Blue, Lichfield Green, Coffee, Nimbus White, Cotswold Blue and Black. Companions were offered in the same colour range, usually with the area around the windows finished in white. Pennant models were available optionally in 'duotone' finish.

ENGINE:

Standard 8, 1953 to 1957 – 803cc, four-cylinder, overhead valve, bore 58mm, stroke 76mm, power 28bhp.

Standard 10, 1954 to 1957 – 948cc, four-cylinder, overhead valve, bore 63mm, stroke 76mm, power 33bhp.

A late model Standard 10 Gold Star showing the opening boot and fuller bumpers fitted to cars from 1957.

The Companion makes a very practical small estate car. Changes to the trim levels of the saloon car were reflected in the estate, with Super, Family and Gold Star versions being available. This example shows the typical duotone finish.

Unlike many other estate cars of the period that had a horizontally split tailgate, the Companion utilised a large side-hinged single door.

More chrome was added to the Standard 8 Gold Star, so the front of the car looks properly finished. The sunroof on this car is an aftermarket enhancement.

Standard 8 'Gold Star' 1957 to 1959 – 803cc, four-cylinder, overhead valve, bore 58mm, stroke 76mm, power 33bhp.
Standard 10 'Gold Star' 1957 to 1959, and Standard Pennant – 948cc, four-cylinder, overhead valve, bore 63mm, stroke 76mm, power 37bhp.
GEARBOX: Four-speed with synchromesh on top three speeds, floor change.
Early models – Overall gearing ratios (all models): 1st 20.9:1, 2nd 11.9:1, 3rd 7.0:1, top 4.9:1, reverse 19.45:1.
'Gold Star' models – Overall gearing ratios (all models): 1st 19.45:1, 2nd 11.2:1, 3rd 6.62:1, top 4.55:1, reverse 19.45:1.
Optional overdrive ratio 1:1.32, operating on all except 1st and reverse gears, giving, effectively, seven forward gears.
Automatic – A proprietary two-pedal control system incorporating a centrifugal clutch was marketed as 'Standrive.' A conventional looking gearlever controlling the usual gears was fitted, but an electrical push switch mounted into the top face of the gear knob was used to electrically operate the clutch while on the move, to allow gear changes to be made.
REAR AXLE: Semi-floating. Ratio 4.9:1 on early cars, 4.55:1 on later.
BRAKES: Hydraulic, operating 7in x 1.5in drums all round.
SUSPENSION: Front: independent with coil springs and double wishbones, telescopic

A larger, more powerful engine, higher level of trim, an opening boot from the outset, and more chrome identified the Standard 10.

27

dampers; rear: live axle, with semi-elliptical springs.

STEERING: Worm and nut.

DIMENSIONS: 8 and 10 saloons – length 142in (3606mm), width 58in (1473mm). **Pennant** – length 148in (3760mm), width 58in (1473mm). **Companion** – 145.5in (3696mm), width 58in (1473mm).

FUEL CAPACITY: 7 gallons (32 litres).

PRODUCTION: In total, 351,727 cars (Standard 8: 136,317, Standard 10: 172,500, Pennant: 42,910).

PERFORMANCE: Early 8s had a top speed of 62mph, later 10s and Pennants could achieve 70mph (manufacturer's figures) with a through the gears acceleration to 50mph being achieved in 18 seconds.

Viewed from the front, this 1959 model 10 Gold Star displays the full grille treatment.

A duotone finish, rear tail fins, hooded headlamps and more chrome turned the rather plain Ten into the stylish Pennant for two years from 1957 until it was replaced in the model range with the Triumph Herald. Similar enhancements were also made to the Companion.

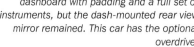

The Pennant featured an improved dashboard with padding and a full set of instruments, but the dash-mounted rear view mirror remained. This car has the optional overdrive.

CHAPTER 6

SIDESCREEN TRS

With the ending of Triumph Roadster production, an opportunity arose for a replacement roadster style car that would appeal to export markets, especially the United States where British sports cars had become extremely popular. The first design by Walter Belgrove, designated TR-X, was shown at the London and Paris Motor Shows in 1950, and despite numerous advanced features and a high specification, failed to meet with approval. This was followed by a requirement to produce a new car for launch at the 1952 London Motor Show with design parameters calling for a top speed of around 90mph and a price of around £500. Following road testing, which revealed poor handling characteristics, a redesign was undertaken and the result was the Triumph TR2.

Sidescreen TRs were provided with simple weather equipment; a folding canvas roof and removable sidescreens were standard on all cars, but a removable hardtop could be specified as an optional extra.

Early cars had long doors that covered the inner sill and could collide with high kerbs making exiting the car difficult. An early modification resulted in a conventional outer sill and short doors being adopted.

TR2

Power for the TR2 came from the ubiquitous Standard wet liner engine, as fitted to the Renown and Vanguard, but now with liners sized to create an engine of 1991cc, keeping it under the two litre limit for competition. Deliveries commenced in July 1953 after a public relations coup for Standard-Triumph earlier in May, when a pre-production TR2 set a speed record of 124.889mph on the Jabbeke Highway in Belgium.

Very early cars were equipped with long doors, rather like early Vanguards; a problem when parked against high kerbs, so a modification to create a shorter door and external sill was implemented.

COLOURS: At launch, the following colours were available: Ice Blue, Geranium, Yellow, White or Black. For 1954, the colour range was modified to include Signal Red, British Racing Green, Geranium, Black or White. **ENGINE:** 1991cc, four-cylinder, overhead valve, bore 83mm, stroke 92mm, power 90bhp.

Opposite and above: A selection of colour schemes available for TR2s. Black, grey and blue were also options. Hardtops when fitted were available in any colour, and weather equipment could also be specified in a wide selection of colours.

GEARBOX: Four-speed with synchromesh on top three speeds, remote floor change. Overall gearing ratios (all models): 1st 12.5:1, 2nd 7.4:1, 3rd 4.9:1, top 3.7:1, reverse 15.8:1. Optional overdrive ratio 1:1.219, operating on top gear only on earliest cars and top three speeds later.

REAR AXLE: Semi-floating. Ratio 3.7:1.

BRAKES: Hydraulic, operating drums all round. Front 10 x 2.25in, rear 9 x 1.75in, increased to 10in from early 1955.

SUSPENSION: Front: independent with coil springs and double wishbones, telescopic dampers; rear: live axle, with semi-elliptical springs and lever arm dampers.

STEERING: Cam and lever.

DIMENSIONS: Length 151in (3835mm), width 55.5in (1410mm).

FUEL CAPACITY: 12.5 gallons (56.8 litres).

PRODUCTION: 8628.

PERFORMANCE: A top speed of 107.3mph (173km/h) and a through-the-gears acceleration time of 11.9 seconds to reach 60mph was recorded during an extended road test by *Motor* magazine in 1954.

TR3

The 1955 Motor Show saw a revised car, the Triumph TR3 on display. Now with a flush radiator grille, stainless steel beading in place of the earlier painted finish, and the option of an occasional rear seat, suitable only for children. Extra power was obtained by cylinder head modifications and larger carburettors to now achieve 95bhp and ultimately 100bhp with further cylinder head revisions. From October 1956, the TR3 was fitted with front disc brakes.

COLOURS: Apple Green, Salvador Blue, Pearl White, Black, Signal Red, British Racing Green.

ENGINE: 1991cc, four-cylinder, overhead valve, bore 83mm, stroke 92mm, power 95bhp, increasing to 100bhp with revised cylinder head.

GEARBOX: As later TR2 with optional overdrive on 2nd, 3rd and top.

BRAKES: Prior to October 1956: Hydraulic, operating drums all round. Front 10 x 2.25in, rear 10 x 1.75in. Later cars: Hydraulic,

With the introduction of the TR3, the frontal appearance of the car was improved.

operating front discs and rear drums. Front 11in diameter discs, rear 10 x 2.25in.

PRODUCTION: 13,377.

PERFORMANCE: Standard-Triumph quoted a top speed of 110mph (177km/h) with 0-60mph acceleration time of 12 seconds. A press car, tested by *Motor* in 1956, achieved a top speed of 105.3mph (169.5km/h) and acceleration of 10.8 seconds.

Other specifications per TR2.

TR3A and TR3B

In January 1958, a further set of modifications saw the TR3 gain a full-width grille, with headlight pods slightly recessed, and conventional door handles now fitted. The manufacturer's name was displayed at

An occasional rear seat became available as an option with the TR3. The roof frame has been completely removed to more clearly show the seating.

Speedometer and rev counter are positioned in clear view of the driver, with minor dials for engine coolant temperature, fuel level, ammeter and oil pressure positioned in the centre. The overdrive switch is to the extreme right of the dashboard, and the fly off handbrake lever sits to the right of the transmission tunnel. The remote gear change lever just clears the lower edge of the dashboard, but enthusiastic gear changes can still result in sore knuckles.

All three variations of front grille treatment can be seen here: TR2 (top), TR3 (centre) and TR3A (lower). TR2s and TR3s had just the Standard-Triumph shield as a bonnet emblem; TR3As gained the maker's name emblazoned in capital letters.

the front of the car. During 1959, a new set of press tools was commissioned, resulting in bodywork detail changes, the most obvious of which being flattened areas around the locations of the boot lid hinges. A new larger engine of 2138cc was also available. Almost immediately, the car was named as the TR3A, but such naming was not to be formally adopted until the very final sidescreen cars appeared specifically for the US market. With the introduction of the successor car, the TR4, dealers in the United States, which was by far the largest market for Triumph, were concerned that the price increase for the new vehicle would restrict sales, and convinced Standard-Triumph to continue the sidescreen cars in limited production, but now fitted with the engine and transmission from the new, TR4, car. These cars were referred to as TR3B.

COLOURS:

TR3A – White, Pale Yellow (Primrose Yellow), British Racing Green, Apple Green, Grey, Powder Blue, Winchester Blue, White, Signal Red.

TR3B – White, Black, Signal Red, Powder Blue.

ENGINE: The higher output 1991cc engine continued to be available as standard, but an optional larger capacity engine was available: 2138cc, four-cylinder, overhead valve, bore 86mm, stroke 92mm, power 100bhp. Other specifications as TR3, except rear brake drums modified to 9 x 1.75in diameter during production run.

For the TR3B, the first 500 cars to be built

The factory hardtop is a simple fit. Recently emerged from a restoration when this photograph was taken, this TR3A shows the detail of the upholstery piping and pleating in the rear cockpit.

were fitted with the 1991cc engine, the remainder with the 2138cc engine. For gearbox details, see TR4 specifications later in this book.

PRODUCTION: TR3A 58,236 TR3B 3331.

PERFORMANCE: The sales brochure claimed a top speed of 110mph and 0-60mph time of 12 seconds. TRs of this era had much success in motorsport, particularly in Alpine Rallying and at Le Mans.

On this early TR2, the simple boot locking mechanism can be seen; just two budget locks requiring a carriage key to open the boot. The spare wheel is stored in a compartment behind the rear number plate, again secured with budget locks. Rear lighting is very simple – a single, central stop lamp, and combined tail lamps and flashing turn signals. The reversing and rear fog lamps are much later additions.

With the TR3A, a locking handle was at last provided to secure the owner's luggage, but the carriage key was still required if the spare wheel needed to be accessed. Rear lighting was modified; amber flashing turn signals (red for certain overseas markets) were now fitted with twin stop and tail lamps. The luggage rack was then, and remains, a popular accessory, especially if the side screens are carried on a touring holiday.

CHAPTER 7

HERALD AND VITESSE

Herald 948

A chance meeting between Standard-Triumph's Engineering Director, Harry Webster, and the talented Italian stylist, Giovanni Michelotti, gave Triumph its distinctive style for the 1960s and 70s. Having proved his ability with the Vanguard face-lift, Michelotti formed a long lasting personal friendship with Webster that was to provide most of Triumph's designs for the remainder of the company's existence. The first complete model to emerge was to be the 1959 Triumph Herald, the model being required to replace the now aging 8 and 10 models. 1959 was a significant time, with the introduction of the Ford Anglia 105E model and BMC Mini also being launched during the year.

The 948cc engine and gearbox from the Pennant were carried over, but whereas the 8 and 10 had been monocoque designs, the Herald reverted to a separate chassis. At the time the car was being finalised, the industry was being reorganised. Standard-Triumph's usual bodywork supplier Fisher & Ludlow was acquired by BMC, and it was clear that they would not be producing pressings for competitors. With no alternatives at the time, the new car was therefore built on a traditional chassis with the bodywork assemblies sourced from Mulliners and Forward Radiator, locally in the Midlands, Hall Engineering in Liverpool, which built the entire front of the car, and Pressed Steel. This turned out to be to Triumph's advantage as the design was to spawn future successful models. Rack and pinion steering was featured, the front suspension continued the wishbone and coil spring system, and the rear suspension was built around a system utilising a transverse leaf spring and swing axles.

Three distinctive body styles were built, all with two doors: a saloon and coupé at the product launch in 1959, and a convertible a year later. The coupé, in keeping with its sporting appearance, featured an engine in a higher state of tune with twin SU

Early Herald models can be identified by the pull handle fitted to the bonnet. The red and white finish suits the car well and represents the style of the cars entered in the 1960 Monte Carlo Rally.

948cc coupé, rear view.

Convertible Herald 948 with period whitewall tyres. The painted bumpers were the original fitting on the early cars.

carburettors. 1961 brought a budget model to market, sold as the Herald S, as a saloon only, and this was to continue in production until 1964; the coupé and convertible were withdrawn in 1961 and the saloon in 1962.

COLOURS: Signal Red, Yellow, Lichfield Green, Power Blue, Monaco Blue, Coffee, Black, White, Targo Purple, Alpine Mauve. Duotone finishes were available and standard for the coupé, usually with white as the contrasting colour although other combinations were possible.

ENGINE: 948cc, four-cylinder, overhead valve, bore 63mm, stroke 76mm, power 34.5bhp. Coupé and cars fitted with option twin carburettors power increased to 42.5bhp.

GEARBOX: Four-speed with synchromesh on top three speeds, remote floor change. Overall gearing ratios: saloon/convertible – 1st 20.82:1, 2nd 11.99:1, 3rd 7.09:1, top 4.875:1, reverse 20.82:1. Coupé – 1st 19.45:1, 2nd 11.2:1, 3rd 6.62:1, top 4.55:1, reverse 20.82:1.

REAR AXLE: Swing axle shafts. Ratio 4.875:1 (saloon/convertible); 4.55:1 (coupé).

BRAKES: Hydraulic, operating drums all round. Front 8 x 1.25in, rear 7 x 1.25in.

SUSPENSION: Front: independent with coil springs and double wishbones, telescopic dampers, anti-roll bar; rear: swing axle, transverse leaf spring, radius rods, telescopic dampers.

STEERING: Rack and pinion.

DIMENSIONS: Length 153in (3886mm), width 60in (1524mm).

FUEL CAPACITY: 7 gallons (32 litres).

PRODUCTION: 100,275 for all 948cc models, including Herald S.

PERFORMANCE: The sales brochure quoted a top speed of 70mph for the saloon and convertible, and 80mph for the coupé. These figures were confirmed by published road tests which also measured a 0-60mph acceleration time of 31 seconds.

Herald 1200 and 12/50

During this period, Standard-Triumph were passing through a serious financial crisis, prior to being acquired by Lancashire-based truck and bus manufacturer, Leyland

Herald 1200 saloons sold well in the 1960s, and can be identified by their rubber bumpers. Solid colours and duotone finishes were available.

Convertible versions of the Herald 1200 were always a popular option.

Herald 12/50 can be easily identified by the full-length factory-fit sunroof.

Motors. A comprehensive review of the model range and future plans resulted in more cash becoming available leading to the launch of the Herald 1200 in 1961, with a revised engine of 1147cc and improved trim. The saloon, coupé and convertible were all continued and a three door estate car was added to the range. Various options were available, including twin carburettors and, from the Autumn of 1961, front disc brakes. 1963 brought an even more luxurious car with more power and a factory fitted full length vinyl sunroof, badged as Herald 12/50.

COLOURS: Throughout the production of the Herald 1200, the range of colours was varied regularly. Some of the more 'exotic' colours such as coffee, purple and mauve were deleted. During the production run, the range included the following: British Racing Green, Lichfield Green, Olive Green, Cactus Green, Cherry Red, Signal Red, Damson Red, Grey, Yellow, Monaco Blue, Powder Blue, Royal Blue, Valencia Blue, Wedgwood Blue. Duotone was a popular option, with the combination of Signal Red and White being especially popular. The estate car was not available in duotone finish.
ENGINE: 1147cc, four-cylinder, overhead valve, bore 69.3mm, stroke 76mm, power

39bhp; (12/50 produced 51bhp from tuned engine with higher compression ratio and revised camshaft.)
GEARBOX: Four-speed with synchromesh on top three speeds, remote floor change. Overall gearing ratios (saloon/convertible): 1st 15.42:1, 2nd 8.88:1, 3rd 5.74:1, top 4.11:1, reverse 15.42:1.
REAR AXLE: Swing axle shafts. Ratio 4.11:1.
BRAKES: Herald 1200 – hydraulic, operating drums all round. Front 8 x 1.25in, rear 7 x 1.25in, except if discs fitted to special order then as 12/50.
Herald 12/50 – Hydraulic, operating front 9in discs and rear drums 7 x 1.25in.
SUSPENSION: As Herald 948.
DIMENSIONS: As Herald 948.
FUEL CAPACITY: 7 gallons (32 litres); estate 9 gallons (41 litres).
PERFORMANCE: Different top speeds were quoted for the various body styles as follows: saloon and convertible: 78mph, coupé: 80mph, estate: 76mph. Similarly, acceleration times varied, for these models shown to 50mph. The coupé was fastest at 16.5 seconds, followed by the convertible at 17 seconds, the saloon at 17.5 seconds and the estate at 18.4 seconds. *Autocar* tested a 1200 saloon in April 1961 and obtained a top speed of 76mph with a 0-50mph acceleration

time of 18.4 seconds, reaching 60mph in 28.6 seconds.

PRODUCTION: Herald 1200 – 289,575 for all body styles, of which nearly 70% were saloons. Herald 12/50 – 53,267.

Herald 13/60

A new model range was announced at the 1967 London Motor Show – the Herald 13/60, comprising saloon, convertible and estate body styles. Now fitted with a 1296cc engine, disc brakes were a standard fitting, the interior trim was further enhanced and, most notably, the front styling of the car was changed by fitting a new bonnet and wing assembly. Saloon, convertible and estate car models remained in production, with the 1200 model continuing until the end of 1970 when all Herald saloon models were withdrawn. Estates and convertibles lasted a few months longer, finally ending some six months later.

COLOURS: Generally, the same as Herald 1200. Damson, White, the darker green shades and Valencia Blue were very popular and suited the car well.

ENGINE: 1296cc, four-cylinder, overhead valve, bore 73.7mm, stroke 76mm, power 61bhp.

GEARBOX: Four-speed with synchromesh on top three speeds, remote floor change. Overall gearing ratios (saloon/convertible): 1st 15.42:1, 2nd 8.88:1, 3rd 5.74:1, top 4.11:1, reverse 15.42:1.

REAR AXLE: Swing axle shafts. Ratio 4.11:1.

BRAKES: Hydraulic, operating front 9in discs and rear drums, 7 x 1.25in.

SUSPENSION: As Herald 948.

DIMENSIONS: As Herald 948.

FUEL CAPACITY: 8.75 gallons (40 litres); estate 9 gallons (41 litres).

PERFORMANCE: The sales brochure boasted a top speed of 85mph for the saloon and convertible or 81-83mph for the estate car. Acceleration was quoted to 50mph and times of 12.0 seconds for the saloon, 11.5 seconds for the convertible and 12.8 seconds for the estate car – a noticeable improvement on the earlier 1200 and 948cc cars. *Motor* tested a saloon in April 1968 and reported the same

With the 13/60 came new sheet metalwork at the front of the car, with revisions to the bonnet and headlamp arrangements. Three body styles were available: saloon, convertible, and estate.

that would be a feature of all Triumph saloons. During the first 18 months that the car was on sale, various modifications to the carburettors were applied to increase power output, eventually reaching a claimed output of 84bhp.

acceleration times to 50mph, 16.6 seconds to reach 60mph and confirmed the top speed claimed in the brochure.

PRODUCTION: 82,650 for all body styles.

Vitesse – a more powerful Herald

Introduced in May 1962 and revitalising a name previously used by Triumph in the 1930s, the Vitesse 6 was a small sporting saloon based on a strengthened Herald chassis, but fitted with a 1596cc six-cylinder engine of similar type to that used in the Vanguard Six. Visually, a new bonnet assembly gave a distinctively angled frontal view with twin headlights. Front disc brakes and larger rear drum brakes were fitted as standard, there was a larger fuel tank and overdrive was a useful option. The car was available as a two-door saloon or convertible. Internally, wooden door cappings matched the wooden dashboard and gave the car an upmarket appearance

COLOURS: As Herald 13/60.

ENGINE: 1596cc, six-cylinder, overhead valve, bore 66.75mm, stroke 76mm, power 70bhp increasing to 84bhp.

GEARBOX: Four-speed all synchromesh, remote floor change.
Overall gearing ratios (saloon/convertible): 1st 12.06:1, 2nd 7.31:1, 3rd 5.16:1, top 4.11:1, reverse 15.42:1. Optional overdrive on 3rd and top with 1:1.25 ratio.

REAR AXLE: Swing axle shafts. Ratio 4.11:1.

BRAKES: Hydraulic, operating front 9in discs and rear drums, 8 x 1.25in.

SUSPENSION: As Herald 13/60.

DIMENSIONS: As Herald 13/60.

FUEL CAPACITY: 9 gallons (41 litres).

PERFORMANCE: The Vitesse 6 was able to achieve a maximum speed of 90mph and accelerate from rest to 60mph in 17 seconds. *Autocar* tested a convertible in September 1965 and reported a top speed of 91mph and 0-60mph acceleration time of 15.5 seconds.

PRODUCTION: 31,260 for both body styles.

First registered in September 1966, this Vitesse 6 dates from just before the original model was replaced with the 2-litre model. Bright bumpers were a feature of the Vitesse.

Vitesse 2-litre

After four years, the Vitesse was enhanced by replacing the unique 1596cc engine with a tuned version of the 2-litre engine fitted to the large 2000 saloon. The gearbox was strengthened, the rear axle ratio changed and new badges showed off the new engine. Production continued until 1968 when it was replaced by the Mark 2 version.

COLOURS: as Herald 13/60.
ENGINE: 1998cc, six-cylinder, overhead valve, bore 74.7mm, stroke 76mm, power 95bhp.
GEARBOX: Four-speed all synchromesh, remote floor change.
Overall gearing ratios (saloon/convertible): 1st 10.31:1, 2nd 6.92:1, 3rd 4.86:1, top 3.89:1, reverse 12.05:1. Optional overdrive on 3rd and top with 1:1.25 ratio.
REAR AXLE: Swing axle shafts. Ratio 3.89:1.
BRAKES: Hydraulic, operating front 9.7in discs and rear drums 8 x 1.25in.
SUSPENSION: As Herald 13/60.
DIMENSIONS: As Herald 13/60.
FUEL CAPACITY: 9 gallons (41 litres).
PERFORMANCE: Triumph's sales brochure claimed a top speed of 100mph and 0-60mph acceleration of 12.5 seconds.
PRODUCTION: 10,830 for both body styles.

Vitesse 2-litre Mark 2

The performance of the 2-litre engine was beginning to overpower the capability of the rear suspension, and the earlier cars developed an unwelcome reputation for poor handling. Triumph addressed this criticism with the Mark 2 which, as well as increasing the engine power even further, was sold with a revised rear suspension now utilising a lower wishbone in conjunction with the transverse leaf spring which remained. Externally, the new car could be identified by the revised horizontal bar grille.

The 2-litre Vitesse now had a new badge boasting of the engine size fitted to the grille. Convertible models of the Vitesse were very popular.

COLOURS: As Herald 13/60.
ENGINE: 1998cc, six-cylinder, overhead valve, bore 74.7mm, stroke 76mm, power 104bhp.
GEARBOX: As Vitesse 2-litre 'Mark 1.'
REAR AXLE: Swing axle shafts. Ratio 3.89:1.

BRAKES: As Vitesse 2-litre Mark 1.
SUSPENSION: Front: as Vitesse 2-litre Mark 1; rear: transverse leaf spring, radius arms, lower wishbones and lever arm dampers.

From the rear, the appearance was very similar to the smaller-engined Herald.

In keeping with many other Triumphs of the period, the Vitesse was tastefully appointed with a real wood dashboard and door cappings, and a comprehensive set of instruments.

DIMENSIONS: As Herald 948.
FUEL CAPACITY: 9 gallons (41 litres).
PERFORMANCE: Triumph's sales brochure for the Mark 2 was quiet on the subject of maximum speed, but emphasised an acceleration time of 11 seconds for the sprint from 0-60mph. In August 1969, *Autocar* published a road test showing a maximum speed of 101mph and 11.9 seconds to achieve 60mph from rest. The new rear suspension was praised as being a notable improvement over the earlier simple swing axle system.
PRODUCTION: 9121 for both body styles.

Mark 2 cars received new badging on the bonnet and a revised grille. Only saloon and convertible versions of the Vitesse were built as production cars, but a handful of special order estates were modified by Triumph's service department in West London.

CHAPTER 8

SPITFIRE AND GT6

Spitfire 4

In the late 1950s, Triumph turned its attention to a small two-seater sports car that could be built on a modified chassis of the newly designed Herald, and styled, again, by Michelotti. Funds were not available for the new car to be put into production until the takeover by Leyland Motors, by which time the Austin-Healey 'frog eye' Sprite had helped to establish the market.

Announced at the 1962 London Motor Show, Spitfire became one of Triumph's best remembered sports cars, and remained in production through various revisions into 1980.

The first car to be introduced was badged as 'Spitfire 4' (not to be confused with the much later Mark 4 Spitfire) and was based on Herald mechanical assemblies, including a mildly retuned twin carburettor engine, transmission and suspension. In common with the Herald, the bonnet and front wings could be lifted as a single assembly to allow easy access to engine and front suspension.

COLOURS: White, Signal Red, Cherry Red, Primrose, Conifer Green, Lichfield Green, Powder Blue, Royal Blue, Wedgwood Blue, Grey, Black.
ENGINE: 1147cc, four-cylinder, overhead valve, bore 69.3mm, stroke 76mm, power 63bhp.
GEARBOX: Four-speed with synchromesh on top three speeds, remote floor change. Overall gearing ratios 1st 15.4:1, 2nd 8.87:1, 3rd 5.73:1, top 4.11:1, reverse 15.4:1.
REAR AXLE: Swing axle shafts. Ratio 4.11:1.
BRAKES: Hydraulic, operating front 9in diameter discs and rear drums 7in x 1.25in.
SUSPENSION: Front: independent with coil springs and double wishbones, telescopic dampers, anti-roll bar; rear: Swing axle, transverse leaf spring, radius rods, telescopic dampers.
STEERING: Rack and pinion.
DIMENSIONS: Length 145in (3760mm), width 57in (1448mm).
FUEL CAPACITY: 9 gallons (41 litres).
PRODUCTION: 45,753.
PERFORMANCE: The original sales brochure quoted a top speed of 'well over 90mph' and 0-60mph acceleration time of 16.5 seconds. Journalist John Bolster writing in a test published in *Autosport* in January 1963 confirmed the top speed, and achieved a 0-60mph acceleration time of 13.2 seconds.

Although bearing a registration mark from 1965, the black mesh grille of this car suggests it is a Spitfire 4.

Spitfire Mark 2

Introduced in 1964, the Mark 2 Spitfire delivered more engine power provided through a revised camshaft gear and a new manifold. Carpets were now provided, and the inner door tops were now trimmed, rather than being finished in body paint colour. As in the case of the Spitfire 4, a heater was still an optional extra, and the roof covering was completely removable. External changes were minimal; the grille was now finished with horizontal bars rather than the mesh of the earlier car.

COLOURS: White, Signal Red, Conifer Green, Royal Blue, Wedgwood Blue, Black.
ENGINE: 1147cc, four-cylinder, overhead valve, bore 69.3mm, stroke 76mm, power 67bhp.
GEARBOX: As Spitfire 4.
REAR AXLE: As Spitfire 4.
BRAKES: As Spitfire 4.
STEERING: As Spitfire 4.
DIMENSIONS: As Spitfire 4.
FUEL CAPACITY: As Spitfire 4.
PRODUCTION: 37,409.
PERFORMANCE: A maximum speed of 96mph and 0-60mph acceleration of 14.8 seconds, according to contemporary reports.

Registered in the same year as the previous image, the revised grille is the most obvious identifying feature of this car being a Spitfire Mk 2.

Rear view of the early Spitfire shows the simple lighting arrangement and clean lines achieved by removing the roof.

Spitfire Mk 2 dashboard view. Some wiring work is being undertaken on this car, and the panel below the main instruments has been cut to allow a radio to be fitted.

Distinctively a Spitfire Mk 3 by the raised front bumper, the pastel and lighter colours in the range suit the little Spitfire. The folding roof is now located under the cover at the rear of the cockpit.

Spitfire Mark 3

1967 brought further changes, resulting in the Spitfire Mark 3. The United States was a strong market for Triumph, and while engine changes to meet emissions and pollution control requirements could be made specifically for that market, it made sense for changes that were mandated to meet safety requirements to be made across the board. Most striking of these changes was the revision to the front bumper, now crossing about halfway up the grille. In addition, a new folding hood was available, and the instrument panel was finished in wood. Under the bonnet, the engine was now the 1296cc unit from the Herald 13/60 in a higher state of tune. Overdrive could be specified as an option, operating on third and top gears. Cars destined for the US were fitted with a less powerful engine to meet emission requirements.

COLOURS: White, Sienna Brown, Damson Red, Signal Red, Jasmine Yellow, Saffron Yellow, Laurel Green, Conifer Green, Royal Blue, Valencia Blue, Wedgwood Blue.
ENGINE: 1296cc, four-cylinder, overhead valve, bore 73.7mm, stroke 76mm, power 75bhp (US models from 1969 onwards 68bhp).
GEARBOX: Four-speed with synchromesh on top three speeds, remote floor change. Overall gearing ratios 1st 15.4:1, 2nd 8.87:1, 3rd 5.73:1, top 4.11:1, reverse 15.4:1.

Having run nearly 2000 miles in 48 hours, these two Spitfire Mk 3s have been participating in a charity event organised by one of the many Triumph clubs. With rain on the horizon, the roof has been raised on both.

Optional overdrive on 3rd and top with 1:1.25 ratio.
All other specifications as Spitfire Mark 2.
PRODUCTION: 65,320.
PERFORMANCE: The UK market brochure quoted a top speed of 100mph, and 0-60mph acceleration time of 12.5 seconds. North American market brochures were rather coy about performance statistics, with no reference to maximum speed, and the nearest to an acceleration figure quoted is the time of 19 seconds for a standing start quarter mile.

Spitfire Mark IV

Branded with Roman numerals to prevent confusion with the first Spitfire 4, the Spitfire Mark IV introduced in 1970 was a radical reskinning of the car, with the restyle again undertaken by Michelotti. The appearance at the front was improved with a black plastic grille and 'under riders,' the wheelarches were flared slightly, the windscreen height was increased by two inches, and a new style of door handles fitted. Along the top of the front wings, the earlier bright chrome strips were deleted, and at the back, above a new, one-piece bumper, sat a Kamm-style tail, matching that fitted to the larger 2000/2500 saloon and Stag. To complete the redesign, a new hardtop could be specified. Inside the cockpit, the instruments

The cleaned-up front wings with the top seam and bright finishing strip removed are a clear identifier for a Spitfire Mk IV. The increased windscreen height can also be seen

The revised shape of the optional hardtop was introduced with the Spitfire Mk IV.

were now in front of the driver, the overdrive control moved to a slide switch in the top of the gearlever knob.

Mechanically, the most significant modification was to the rear suspension. Responding to criticism of the handling resulting from the swing axle rear suspension, rather than add the lower rear wishbones in the manner used to address the issues with the Vitesse, a modification was made to the rear transverse spring mounting, so that now just a single leaf was fixed to the differential casing allowing the remaining spring leaves free to pivot.

In 1973, a larger 1500cc engine with a single carburettor was fitted to US market cars.

COLOURS: White, Sienna Brown, Carmine Red, Damson Red, Pimento Red, Signal Red, Mimosa Yellow, Saffron Yellow, Emerald Green, Laurel Green, French Blue, Sapphire Blue, Valencia Blue, Wedgwood Blue, Mallard Blue, Magenta.
ENGINE: 1296cc, four-cylinder, overhead valve, bore 73.7mm, stroke 76mm, power 63bhp DIN (US models 1971 year: 58bhp, 1972 year: 48bhp).
US market only from 1973: 1493cc, four-cylinder, overhead valve, bore 73.7mm, stroke 87.5mm, power 57bhp DIN.
GEARBOX: Four-speed with synchromesh on all speeds, remote floor change.

With the larger engine fitted, the last cars in the Spitfire range carried 'Spitfire 1500' badges, now in the form of vinyl decals.

Overall gearing ratios 1st 13.65:1, 2nd 8.41:1, 3rd 5.41:1, top 3.89:1, reverse 15:1.
Optional overdrive on 3rd and top with 1:1.25 ratio.
US models 1972 onward: Four-speed with synchromesh on all speeds, remote floor change.
Overall gearing ratios 1st 14.4:1, 2nd 8.87:1, 3rd 5.71:1, top 4.11:1, reverse 16.39:1.
Optional overdrive on 3rd and top with 1:1.25 ratio.
REAR AXLE: Swing axle shafts. Ratio 3.89:1 (4.11:1 for US models, 1972 model year onwards).
SUSPENSION: Front: independent with coil springs and double wishbones, telescopic dampers, anti-roll bar; rear: swing axle, transverse leaf spring (now with only lower leaf attached to differential case), radius rods, telescopic dampers.
DIMENSIONS: Length 149in (3785mm), width 58.5in (1486mm).
FUEL CAPACITY: 7.25 gallons (33 litres).
All other specifications as Spitfire Mark 3.
PRODUCTION: 70,021.
PERFORMANCE: A top speed of 95mph and 0-60mph time of 14.5 seconds according to the sales brochure. A short item in *Motorsport* from January 1971 described the car as a 'toy racer' with a top speed of just under 100mph and 0-60mph acceleration time of 12.5 seconds.

Spitfire 1500

From December 1974, the 1500cc engine was introduced to all markets to create the Spitfire 1500 model. The longer bore of the larger engine increased its torque, thus making it more flexible to drive in traffic. Minor changes occurred during the final years of Spitfire production. Following fashion, and what was said to be a safety improvement, many of the brightly finished items such as windscreen wipers, door handles and mirrors were now finished in matt black. Steering column switches were modernised, and the vinyl seats were updated with a partial cloth finish in a houndstooth check pattern. Tightening emissions regulations in California made it impossible to sell the car in that State,

47

a sales territory that was at the time responsible for significant volumes of the production, and with the ensuing loss of volume, the car became uneconomic to manufacture. Accordingly, production finally ended after 18 years in August 1980, with the final car off the assembly line being retained for posterity.

This red example also has the 'Spitfire 1500' vinyl decals.

COLOURS: The colour range for the Spitfire 1500 changed on an almost annual basis. The following colours were available for all or some of the production period: White, Russet Brown, Maple Brown, Vermillion Red, Carmine Red, Pimento Red, Flamenco Red, Topaz (orange), Inca Yellow, Mimosa Yellow, Java Green, British Racing Green, Brooklands Green, French Blue, Delft Blue, Pageant Blue, Tahiti Blue,

ENGINE: 1493cc, four-cylinder, overhead valve, bore 73.7mm, stroke 87.5mm, power 71bhp DIN (US models 57bhp).

GEARBOX: Four-speed with synchromesh on all speeds, remote floor change.
Overall gearing ratios 1st 12.7:1, 2nd 7.84:1, 3rd 5.05:1, top 3.63:1, reverse 14:1.
Optional overdrive on 3rd and top with 1:1.25 ratio.
US models: Four-speed with synchromesh on all speeds, remote floor change.
Overall gearing ratios 1st 13.66:1, 2nd 8.41:1, 3rd 5.41:1, top 3.89:1, reverse 15:1.
Optional overdrive on 3rd and top with 1:1.25 ratio.

REAR AXLE: Swing axle shafts. Ratio 3.63:1 (3.89:1 for US models).
All other specifications as Spitfire Mark IV.

PRODUCTION: 70,021.

PERFORMANCE: UK specification cars boasted a maximum speed of 100mph and acceleration from 0-60mph of 11.3 seconds, according to the sales brochure. For US specification cars, a top speed of 93mph and 0-60mph acceleration time of 13.5 seconds.

On later cars, Mk IV and 1500, the instruments were positioned directly in front of the driver. This car is fitted with the optional overdrive, operated via a toggle switch on the gear knob.

GT6 Mark 1

Michelotti was commissioned by Standard-Triumph to produce a fastback GT version of his earlier Spitfire design. The additional weight required more power than that which could be provided by the current Spitfire's

This rear three-quarter view shows the lack of ventilation grilles in the Mark 1 body of the GT6.

1147cc engine, and so the project was not taken forward. But the overall design did form the basis of the glass fibre bodywork used for the class-winning Spitfire GT cars raced at Le Mans. Eventually, combining the 2-litre engine from the Vitesse with the mechanical elements of the Spitfire, a new car, the GT6, emerged in 1966. With a fastback design and opening rear hatch, the car quickly became known as 'the poor man's [Jaguar] E-type.' One drawback in the early cars was the rear suspension, based on the original swing axle design from the Vitesse, which, coupled with the heavier engine, could give difficult handling, and this came in for much criticism until rectified in the Mark 2 version that followed.

COLOURS: White, Wedgwood Blue, Royal Blue, Signal Red, Conifer Green.
ENGINE: 1998cc, six-cylinder, overhead valve, bore 74.7mm, stroke 76mm, power 95bhp.
GEARBOX: Four-speed with synchromesh on top three speeds, remote floor change. Overall gearing ratios 1st 8.66:1, 2nd 5.82:1, 3rd 4.11:1, top 3.27:1, reverse 10.13:1. Optional overdrive on 3rd and top with 1:1.25 ratio.
REAR AXLE: Swing axle shafts. Ratio 3.27:1.
BRAKES: Hydraulic, operating front 9.7in diameter discs and rear drums 8in x 1.25in.
SUSPENSION: Front: independent with coil springs and double wishbones, telescopic dampers, anti-roll bar; rear: Swing axle, transverse leaf spring, radius rods, telescopic dampers.
STEERING: Rack and pinion.
DIMENSIONS: Length 145in (3683mm), width 57in (1448mm).
FUEL CAPACITY: 9.75 gallons (44.3 litres).
PRODUCTION: 15,818.
PERFORMANCE: Manufacturer's figures show a maximum speed of 106mph and acceleration through the gears to reach 60mph in 12 seconds. A road-test by *CAR* magazine, published in October 1967, confirmed the top speed, but achieved a faster acceleration time of 10.7 seconds.

Mark 1 GT6s shared a similar front to the Spitfire of the same period. The registration of this actual car suggests that it has been retrofitted with an earlier front.

GT6 Mark 2

Two years into production, a number of weaknesses in the original car were addressed with the GT6 Mark 2, marked as GT6+ in North America. The rear suspension was revised, with the addition of lower wishbones in the same manner as for the Vitesse, and through-flow ventilation was provided to overcome a common complaint that the original car suffered badly from interior steaming up and stuffiness. Externally, the front bumper was raised in the same manner as the Mark 2 Spitfire. Under the bonnet, a revised cylinder head provided for additional power and thus a higher maximum speed. However, emissions

The front was revised for the Mark 2, again with similarities to the treatment of the Spitfire.

regulations meant reduced power output for cars destined for the US market.

COLOURS: White, Wedgwood Blue, Royal Blue, Valencia Blue, Signal Red, Conifer Green, Jasmine Yellow. Damson Red and Sienna Brown were added as options in late 1969, while Conifer Green was replaced with Laurel Green, and later Saffron Yellow was made available.
ENGINE: 1998cc, six-cylinder, overhead valve, bore 74.7mm, stroke 76mm, power 105bhp (95bhp for US GT6+ model).
SUSPENSION: Front: independent with coil springs and double wishbones, telescopic dampers, anti-roll bar; rear: swing axle, transverse leaf spring, lower wish bones, radius rods, telescopic dampers.
All other specifications as GT6 Mark 1.
PRODUCTION: 12,066.
PERFORMANCE: Manufacturer's figures show the maximum speed was increased to 110mph but acceleration through the gears to reach 60mph was now 10.5 seconds. *Autocar* printed a road test in April 1969 and achieved a maximum speed of 107mph and acceleration time of 10 seconds.

Rear styling of a Mark 2 GT6 showing the top hinged rear tailgate. The additional ventilation now fitted to the rear quarter panels is visible.

GT6 interior. The two or instrument dials in the passenger side below the dashboard are not a standard fitting, although the 'fluffy dice' were a common accessory of the period.

GT6 Mark 3

Rationalisation of production with the Spitfire resulted in the GT6 Mark 3. The front was revised with a higher bumper and 'under riders,' the wing tops lost their brightwork embellishment, and the windscreen height was revised. At the rear, the tail was revised in common with the Spitfire, while further engine improvements increased engine output still further. Inside the car, the overdrive switch, when fitted, was now placed in the centre of the gear change knob. In common with the Spitfire suspension revisions, for the final year of GT6 production the rear suspension was modified again using the 'swing spring' arrangement of later Spitfires.

COLOURS: GT6 Mark 3 colours were changed regularly; initially the following were available: White, Wedgwood Blue, Sapphire Blue, Valencia Blue, Laurel Green, Signal Red, Damson, Saffron, Sienna Brown. In January

1972, this was simplified to: White, Sapphire Blue, Emerald Green, Pimento Red, Damson, Saffron, Sienna Brown. Later in 1972 the colour range was further revised to now include: White, Sapphire Blue, French Blue, Mallard Green, Emerald Green, Carmine Red, Pimento Red, Sienna Brown. Finally, from approximately February 1973, the following colours were available: White, Sapphire Blue, French Blue, Emerald Green, Mallard Green, Carmine Red, Pimento Red, Magenta, Mimosa Yellow, Sienna Brown.
ENGINE: 1998cc, six-cylinder, overhead valve, bore 74.7mm, stroke 76mm, power 105bhp (US models, 1971: 90bhp, 1972 and 1973: 79bhp).
SUSPENSION: Front: independent with coil

springs and double wishbones, telescopic dampers, anti-roll bar; rear: as GT6 Mark 2 except for 1973 model year: swing axle, transverse leaf spring with only lower leaf fixed to differential casing, radius rods, telescopic dampers.

All other specifications as GT6 Mark 1.

PRODUCTION: 13,042.

PERFORMANCE: Maximum speed was again increased slightly to 112mph with 10.1 seconds required to accelerate from rest to 60mph.

Again, in keeping with the modifications made to the front of the Spitfire, Mark 3 GT6s also gained a set of smoothed front wings. XJH is finished in Magenta; a colour very much of the period …

… and a revised rear that adopted the Triumph 'house style.'

CHAPTER 9

MICHELOTTI TRS

TR4

Replacing the successful sidescreen TR was not going to be simple. A number of designs were prototyped, but it was again a style by Michelotti that was chosen and brought to market as TR4 in 1961. Built on a strengthened, modified chassis, now with rack and pinion steering, and providing such creature comforts as wind-up windows, the TR4 was powered by the 2138cc wet liner engine carried over from earlier Standard-Triumph cars. The TR4 was supplied as a roadster, with removable soft roof, or as a coupé with an innovative removable hardtop. When this was specified, a rear windscreen was fitted to the rear decking with a removable metal roof panel bridging front and rear windscreens. As this was too large to be carried in the car, a folding frame and soft top was provided. Because of the similarity to the traditional horse carriage, this style of roof was known as a 'Surrey.'

Radically different to the side screen TRs that preceded it, the TR4 was a stylish car when new, and remains so today.

COLOURS: White, Powder Blue, Wedgwood Blue, British Racing Green, Conifer Green, Signal Red, Black
ENGINE: 2138cc, four-cylinder, overhead valve, bore 86mm, stroke 92mm, power 100bhp, or optionally.
1991cc, four-cylinder, overhead valve, bore 83mm, stroke 92mm, power 100bhp.
GEARBOX: Four-speed with synchromesh on all forward speeds, remote floor change. Overall gearing ratios 1st 11.61:1, 2nd 7.43:1, 3rd 4.9:1, top 3.7:1, reverse 11.92:1. Optional overdrive on 3rd and top with 1:1.23 ratio.
REAR AXLE: Semi-floating. Ratio 3.7:1 (4.1:1 when overdrive fitted).
BRAKES: Hydraulic, operating front 10.9in diameter discs and rear drums 9in x 1.75in.
SUSPENSION: Front: independent with coil springs and double wishbones, telescopic dampers; rear: live axle, with semi-elliptical springs and lever arm dampers.
STEERING: Rack and pinion.
DIMENSIONS: Length 154in (3912mm), width 57.5in (1460mm).
FUEL CAPACITY: 11.7 gallons (53.1 litres).
PRODUCTION: 40,253.
PERFORMANCE: The original sales brochure quoted a top speed of 110mph and 0-50mph acceleration time of 8.2 seconds. *Autocar* tested a TR4 in January 1962 and reported a maximum speed of 104mph with 0-60mph acceleration of 10.9 seconds.

The instrument layout was not changed much from the TR3A, and the 'fly-off' lever handbrake was retained. Early TR4s featured a dashboard finished in white paint.

TR4A

The rear suspension of the TR4, carried over from the earlier TRs, came in for criticism. The solution was to incorporate the rear suspension system from the large 2000 saloon using semi trailing arms and coil springs to create the TR4A, which was introduced during 1965. Other changes were made: the handbrake, still of the 'fly-off' variety, was repositioned to sit on top of the transmission tunnel, the front indicator lamps were now positioned towards the top of the front wings, at the end of a stylistic side embellishment, and the cars were badged as TR4A IRS (IRS – independent rear suspension). On the bonnet, the traditional shield badge was replaced with a Triumph globe. Representation from the dealer network convinced Standard-Triumph that the older suspension system should be continued for the North American market, but, as further production of the old TR4 chassis was no longer possible, additional brackets were grafted on to the new chassis to allow the semi-elliptical springs to be retained.

COLOURS: White, Royal Blue, Wedgwood Blue, British Racing Green, Conifer Green, Signal Red, Black.
ENGINE: 2138cc, four-cylinder, overhead valve, bore 86mm, stroke 92mm, power 104bhp.
REAR AXLE: Differential mounted to chassis, sliding joint drive shafts. Ratio as TR4.
SUSPENSION: Front: independent with coil springs and double wishbones, telescopic dampers; rear: independent using semi-training arms, coil springs and lever arm dampers.
For US market only, optionally as TR4.

With the TR4A, chromed embellishers were fitted to the front wings that incorporated side lights and turn signals. A folding hood was now fitted.

TR4A with hood raised for weather protection.

DIMENSIONS: Length 154in (3912mm), width 58in (1473mm).
All other specifications as TR4.
PRODUCTION: 28,465.
PERFORMANCE: Maximum speed, according to the sales brochure, remained at 110mph, but 0-50mph acceleration time of 7.9 seconds. *Autocar* tested a TR4A in May 1965 and reported a maximum speed of 109mph with 0-60mph acceleration of 11.4 seconds.

The Surrey roof was popular, giving the benefit of open air motoring and protection from buffeting drafts. Here, a Surrey-fitted car is shown with roof open.

TR5/TR250

It became clear that more power was required to remain competitive, and that development of the wet liner engine had been taken as far as possible. Enlarging the six-cylinder engine, as fitted to the Vitesse, 2000 and GT6, by increasing its stroke and adding the Lucas petrol injection system, resulted in a significant increase in power. It was promoted as the first British production sports car to be fitted with petrol injection (PI). However, Triumph development engineers were not confident in meeting the increasingly tighter US emission rules, and instead fitted twin carburettors to cars destined for the US market, selling it as the Triumph TR250 with different detailed badging and a unique racing strip across the bonnet and front wings. Launched in 1967, the TR5/TR250 was built for just over a year before being replaced by the TR6.

COLOURS: White, Royal Blue, Valencia Blue, Conifer Green, Signal Red, Jasmine Yellow.

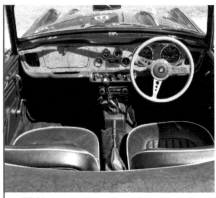

TR4A now had a real wood dashboard, and the handbrake, still a fly-off type, was relocated to the top of the transmission tunnel.

A metal roof panel could be fitted between the windscreen rail and the top of the rear screen, providing all the benefits of a hardtop for Surrey models. As the metal panel was too large to fit in the boot, a vinyl cover, fitting over a metal subframe, was provided to give protection from inclement weather, and this could easily fit in the car.

A TR5 with folding roof.

A TR5 fitted with Surrey roof. Although at first glance the body appears to be the same as a TR4A, there are many detail differences: badges, revised front grille, rear side marker lamps, and repositioned door locks. (Both TR5s shown are fitted with aftermarket 'Minilite' wheels.)

Wearing its distinctive bonnet 'go faster stripes,' this TR250 is fitted with the correct style wheel trims, though has replacement mirrors.

ENGINE: 2498cc, six-cylinder, overhead valve, bore 74.7mm, stroke 95mm, power 150bhp (gross), 142bhp (nett) (PI equipped cars), 104bhp (carburettor equipped cars for US market).

GEARBOX: Four-speed with synchromesh on all forward speeds, remote floor change. Overall gearing ratios 1st 10.83:1, 2nd 6.94:1, 3rd 4.59:1, top 3.45:1, reverse 11.11:1. Optional overdrive on 2nd, 3rd and top with 1:1.22 ratio.

REAR AXLE: Ratio 3.45:1.

BRAKES: Hydraulic, operating front 10.9in diameter discs and rear drums 9in x 1.75in. Servo assistance now fitted as standard.
All other specifications as TR4A.

FUEL CAPACITY: 11.25 gallons (51 litres).

PRODUCTION: TR5 2947, TR250 8484.

PERFORMANCE: Maximum speed, according to the sales brochure was increased to 125mph, although with a caveat that noise restrictions in certain markets may reduce this to 115mph. Brochure acceleration was still specified to 50mph, and the time quoted was 6.5 seconds. *Motor* road tested the car in France during May 1968, and achieved a maximum speed of 117.2mph. Acceleration to 60mph was timed at 8.1 seconds.

The TR5 featured Triumph's petrol-injected engine; the first for any volume production car.

CHAPTER **10**

TRIUMPH 2000

With sales of the Vanguard and Ensign rapidly dwindling, and the car being outclassed in the market, Standard-Triumph needed a radical new car as a replacement if it were to continue as a successful player in the medium to large car segment. Early in-house designs were not inspiring, and so, aided by the injection of cash from Leyland Motors' purchase of Standard-Triumph, it was again Michelotti who came up with a pleasing design that set the style for Triumph saloon cars for the future, and which defined a new market segment. Rover, arch rival in the same market space, was working on a car to replace its equally aged P4 models, and the new Triumph 2000 and Rover 2000 were to be keen competitors in the market. Both offered interior appointments and performance that were more common in the class above, but went about it in different ways. Triumph offered a six-cylinder engine against the Rover's four, Triumph's construction was relatively conventional whereas Rover shared concepts with the Citroën DS, and Triumph provided fully independent rear suspension. Both cars were first seen in public at the London Motor Show of 1963, and both would last well into the late 1970s.

COLOURS: The following selection were available for some or all of the period: White, Jasmine, Wedgwood Blue, Valencia Blue, Royal Blue, Conifer Green, Cherry Red, Signal Red, Damson, Olive Green, Cactus Green, Grey, Black. Early 2000s were also available in duotone colours.
ENGINE: 1998cc, six-cylinder, twin carburettors, overhead valve, bore 74.7mm, stroke 76mm, power 90bhp.
GEARBOX: Four-speed with synchromesh on all forward speeds, remote floor change. Overall gearing ratios 1st 13.45:1, 2nd 8.61:1, 3rd 5.64:1, top 4.1:1, reverse 13.81:1. Optional overdrive on 3rd and top with 1:1.22 ratio. Optional three-speed automatic (Borg Warner model 35) with torque converter and floor mounted shift.

An early example of a Triumph 2000 finished in black over cactus. Early cars were fitted with larger bumper over-riders.

Three exemplary later Triumph 2000s in a range of colours. Rubber inserts were fitted to the over-riders as production neared its end.

From the rear, the Triumph 2000 epitomised a crisp style that became a common feature across the entire product range. The centre badge on the bumper shows the car as a 2000, and the small badge below the maker's insignia boasts that this car is fitted with overdrive.

An opulent interior of real wood and leather was used in the 2000.

Overall gearing ratios 1st 8.84:1, 2nd 5.37:1, top 3.7:1, reverse 7.73:1.

REAR AXLE: Differential mounted to rear subframe, sliding joint drive shafts. Ratio 4.1:1 (3.7:1 when automatic gearbox fitted).

BRAKES: Hydraulic, operating front 9.75in diameter discs and rear drums 9in x 1.75in. Servo assisted.

SUSPENSION: Front: independent with MacPherson strut and coil spring, telescopic dampers; rear: independent using semi-trailing arms, coil springs and telescopic dampers.

STEERING: Rack and pinion.

DIMENSIONS: Length 173.75in (4413mm), width 65in (1651mm).

FUEL CAPACITY: 14 gallons (63.6 litres).

PRODUCTION: 113,157.

PERFORMANCE: According to the sales brochure, the maximum speed quoted was 95mph, with an acceleration time to 60mph of 13.6 seconds. A road test by *Motor*, published in March 1964 confirmed the acceleration time, but slightly bettered the maximum speed by recording a best of 97.6mph.

2000 estate

An estate car followed for 1965. Unusually for an estate car of the period, the Triumph 2000 estate was fitted with the same quality level of trim as the saloon. The rear load compartment was accessed by a one-piece top-hinged tailgate, again, unusual, as most saloon-derived estates continued to use a split tailgate design.

Specifications for the estate remained as for the saloon, except for the standard fit of radial ply tyres (optional on the saloon) and a reduction in fuel tank capacity to 11.5 gallons (52.3 litres). A top speed of 92mph and acceleration to 60mph time of 14.9 seconds were quoted.

Minor updates followed in late 1966 with full-flow ventilation, revised dials for the speedometer and minor dial cluster. Externally, the bumper over-riders were given a rubber insert.

A left-hand drive 2000 estate exported to France and still regularly used. The larger over-riders indicate that this is a very early estate model.

Triumph 2.5 PI

A significant change came in October 1968 when the Triumph 2.5 PI was announced. Using a mildly de-tuned engine from the TR5, complete with the petrol injection system, Triumph claimed this as the first British built saloon car to be fitted with petrol injection. Externally, the PI cars could be recognised by black vinyl covered rear 'C' posts fitted with a circular PI badge, the bonnet top vent was now adorned with a badge displaying 'injection' and rear badges also boasted of the increased engine capacity and injection. Shortly afterwards an estate version of the injected car followed.

COLOURS: As 2000.
ENGINE: 2498cc, six-cylinder, Lucas petrol injection, overhead valve, bore 74.7mm, stroke 95mm, power 132bhp.
GEARBOX: Four-speed with synchromesh on all forward speeds, remote floor change.
Overall gearing ratios 1st 11.32:1, 2nd 7.25:1, 3rd 4.78:1, top 3.45:1, reverse 11.62:1.
Optional overdrive on 3rd and top with 1:1.22 ratio.
Optional three speed automatic (Borg Warner model 35) with torque converter and floor mounted shift.
Overall gearing ratios 1st 8.84:1, 2nd 5.37:1, top 3.7:1, reverse 7.73:1. Oil cooler fitted as standard on automatic.
REAR AXLE: As 2000 except ratio 3.45:1 (3.7:1 when automatic gearbox fitted).
BRAKES: As 2000.
SUSPENSION: As 2000.
STEERING: Rack and pinion.
DIMENSIONS: As 2000.
FUEL CAPACITY: Saloon: 14 gallons (63.6 litres); estate: 11.5 gallons (52.3 litres).
PRODUCTION: Saloon: 8658; estate: 371.
PERFORMANCE: Triumph claimed a maximum speed of 110mph and 0-60mph acceleration time of 10.5 seconds. A published road test by *Autocar* in February 1969 could only achieve 107mph, with 10.4 seconds needed to reach 60mph.

Two pristine examples of Triumph's petrol-injected 2.5-litre car, which was a very fast and comfortable form of transport. In common with many of these cars, neither has retained its original wheels.

Mark 2 saloon and estate
2000, 2500 and 2.5 PI models

Using some of the visual aspects of the two-door Grand Tourer design that would become the Triumph Stag, the Mark 2 version of the big saloon was placed on sale for 1969. The centre section of the car was retained, now fitted with a longer bonnet and boot. The interior was completely revamped with a new wood veneer dashboard with all the minor controls mounted on the steering column. At the rear of the car, the larger boot was now accessed by a flat lid over a large sill, resulting in the estate car being a hybrid of the revised front and original rear. Under the bonnet, the 2000 gained a new cylinder head. In late 1974, the range was face-lifted. Obvious visual changes to the face-lifted cars included a revised front grille, and rubber strips fitted to the chrome bumpers. A new twin carburettor 2500 was introduced, the PI became the Triumph 2500 Injection, and was quickly withdrawn entirely, with the remaining models now badged as 2000TC and 2500TC. Finally, a range topping model badged as 2500S was introduced in both saloon and estate styles.

COLOURS: Colour changes occurred regularly with considerable overlap. The following were available for all or part of the time following the introduction of the Mark 2 and prior to the face-lift models going on sale: White, Carmine

Early Mark 2 cars showing the revised front styling, and a selection of the colours available.

Red, Pimento Red, Damson, Sienna Brown, Wedgwood Blue, Ice Blue, Valencia Blue, Royal Blue, Sapphire Blue, French Blue, Saffron, Mimosa (yellow), Honeysuckle, Conifer Green, Laurel Green, Emerald Green, Grey.

With the introduction of the face-lift models, new colours reflected the fashion of the mid 1970s, and the following were available: White, Carmine Red, Maple Brown, Russet Brown, Mimosa, Topaz, Inca Yellow, British Racing Green, Java Green, French Blue, Delft Blue, Tahiti Blue.

ENGINE:

2000 models – 1998cc, six-cylinder, twin carburettors, overhead valve, bore 74.7mm, stroke 76mm, power 84bhp (DIN); 2000TC power 91bhp (DIN).

2.5 PI models – 2498cc, six-cylinder, Lucas petrol injection, overhead valve, bore 74.7mm, stroke 95mm, power 124bhp (DIN).

2500 models – 2498cc, six-cylinder, twin carburettors, overhead valve, bore 74.7mm, stroke 95mm, power 99bhp (DIN) 1974 and 75 models, power 106bhp (DIN) later 2500TC and 2500S models.

GEARBOX:

2000 models – four-speed with synchromesh on all forward speeds, remote floor change. Overall gearing ratios 1st 13.45:1, 2nd 8.61:1, 3rd 5.64:1, top 4.1:1, reverse 13.81:1. Optional overdrive (revised) on 3rd and top with 1:1.25 ratio.

2500 models – four-speed with synchromesh on all forward speeds, remote floor change. Overall gearing ratios 1st 11.32:1, 2nd 7.25:1, 3rd 4.78:1, top 3.45:1, reverse 11.62:1. Optional overdrive (revised) on 3rd and top with 1:1.25 ratio.

Optional three-speed automatic (Borg Warner model 35 prior to face-lifted models, BW65 introduced thereafter) with torque converter and floor mounted shift. Overall gearing ratios 1st 8.84:1, 2nd 5.37:1, top 3.7:1, reverse 7.73:1.

Although the general shape of the car was retained for the Mark 2 version, the boot was extended, and now opened over a high sill, rather than the lid extending to the rear bumper. The 'sunflower' wheel trims fitted are original.

For the Mark 2 PI, a black anodised grille bearing a badge boasting '2500 Injection' was fitted. This car shows the original wheel trims and correct profile tyres. The colour appears to be Valencia Blue, which was the shade that Triumph chose to illustrate the sales brochure for this car.

The estate car continued in Mark 2 form, but was a hybrid of a Mark 2 front grafted onto a Mark 1 rear, creating a unique situation where the estate car was actually shorter than the equivalent saloon. Nevertheless, the car remained a stylish load hauler. This example is fitted with PI wheel trims.

In face-lift form, these cars illustrate the final form of the big saloon, and a variety of fashionable colours from the later 1970s. A revised radiator grille and rubber insert to the chrome bumpers are the obvious changes.

Mark 2 face-lift PI cars were only built in small numbers prior to being replaced by the new range-topping 2500S model. Here is a rare survivor.

REAR AXLE: Differential mounted to rear subframe, sliding joint drive shafts. Ratio 4.1:1 for 2000 models, and 3.45:1 for 2500 models (3.7:1 when automatic gearbox fitted).

BRAKES: As Mark 1 models, except for thicker front discs. PI models fitted with vacuum reservoir for servo.

SUSPENSION: As Mark 1 cars, except for wider rear axle width on Mark 2 cars with

61

modified trailing arms, and revised spring rates for later cars.

STEERING: As Mark 1, power steering now available.

DIMENSIONS: Saloon: length 182.28in (4630mm), width 66.5in (1689mm), 'face-lift' models length 183.5in (4661mm), width 67.25in (1708mm). Estate: length 177in (4496mm), width 66.5in (1689mm), 'face-lift' models length 178.5in (4534mm), width 67.25in (1708mm).

FUEL CAPACITY: 14 gallons (63.6 litres) for saloon and 12.75 gallons (58 litres) for estate.

PRODUCTION: 2000 saloon and estate:

186,672; 2.5 PI and 2500 Injection, saloon and estate: 47,455; 2500TC and S, saloon and estate: 40,353.

PERFORMANCE: The figures published in the 1974 TC model brochure ranged from 93mph to 103mph for maximum speed and 0-60mph acceleration times varying from 15.1 seconds to 12.0 seconds. The statistics for the Mark 2 PI car were more exciting with a maximum speed of 108mph and acceleration time of 11 seconds to 60mph being quoted. *Motor* tested a 2.5 PI Mark 2 in October 1969, and provided figures of 117.6mph and 9.7 seconds to reach 60mph.

All Mark 2 models were fitted with a revised dashboard, and controls that were widely praised for their ergonomics. The original 2000 and face-lift 2000TC and 2500TC models received a simple set of instruments, while the PI and 2500S models were fitted with a comprehensive set of dials that would not be out of place in one of Triumph's sports models.

CHAPTER 11

1300 TO DOLOMITE

Triumph 1300

Thoughts were turned to replacing the Herald with a new model, code named "AJAX," that would sell at roughly the same price and serve much the same market. The new car would be built on a monocoque structure and feature front-wheel drive following the success of BMC's Mini and 1100 models. But instead of placing the engine across the car with the gearbox situated in the sump, Triumph's design placed the engine longitudinally, positioning the gearbox below and behind the engine, with the final drive underneath the sump. Body styling was again by Michelotti, resulting in a final design that had the appearance of the smaller 2000, with a similar quality interior, and independent suspension all round. Again, in keeping with the large car, the name chosen to market the car reflected its engine capacity, and the Triumph 1300 was announced in October 1965 with first customer deliveries in January 1966.

Triumph's 1300 shares many styling features with the larger 2000, both cars having been styled by Michelotti.

The rear view shares similarities with the larger model, too.

COLOURS: The following is a selection of the colours available: White, Wedgwood Blue, Valencia Blue, Royal Blue, Olive Green, Conifer Green, Signal Red, Cherry Red, Grey.
ENGINE: 1296cc, four-cylinder, overhead valve, bore 73.7mm, stroke 76mm, power 61bhp.
GEARBOX: Four-speed with synchromesh on all forward speeds. Overall gearing ratios 1st 13.97:1, 2nd 8.87:1, 3rd 5.96:1, top 4.37:1, reverse 16.39:1.
FRONT-WHEEL DRIVE SYSTEM: Differential mounted below sump, drive shafts with flexible couplings. Differential ratio 4.11:1.
BRAKES: Hydraulic, operating front 8.75in diameter discs and rear drums 8in x 1.25in.
SUSPENSION: Front: independent with double wishbones and coil springs, telescopic dampers; rear: independent using semi-trailing arms, coil springs and telescopic dampers.
STEERING: Rack and pinion.

Boot space is larger than might be anticipated, given the short rear overhang, although access can be difficult.

DIMENSIONS: Length 155in (3937mm), width 61.75in (1569mm).
FUEL CAPACITY: 11.75 gallons (53.4 litres).
PRODUCTION: 113,008 (35,342 1300TC).
PERFORMANCE: The sales brochure quoted a maximum speed of 85mph, and through the gears acceleration time to 60mph of 18.5 seconds. The magazine *CAR* performed a road test, published in March 1966, recording a 0-60mph acceleration time of 17.7 seconds, and maximum speed of 87mph.

TRIUMPH 1300TC

Very few changes were made to the 1300 during its production life, except for the introduction of the higher performance twin carburettor for the Triumph 1300TC during 1967, now claiming an output of 75bhp, and fitted with a brake servo as standard. A test by *CAR*, published some two years after the earlier test, reported an increased maximum speed of 91mph, and 0-60mph acceleration time of 15.5 seconds. Both cars continued in production alongside each other until 1970. The plan to replace the Herald family with the 1300 never came to fruition, with the last of the Heralds continuing in production very slightly longer than the model which had been intended to replace it.

TRIUMPH 1500

Introduced in 1970, the Triumph 1500 took the basic design concept of the 1300 and combined this with a longer front, now incorporating twin headlamps, and extended boot. The interior was reworked to now have a resemblance to the Mark 2 versions of the larger 2000 models. A brake servo was now standard, but the rear suspension was significantly revised, with a beam axle replacing the earlier, fully independent system.

COLOURS: The following colours were available on the 1500 for all or some of the period of production: Pimento Red, Signal Red, Damson, White, Sapphire Blue, Royal Blue, Wedgwood Blue, Mallard, Valencia Blue, Emerald Green, Laurel Green, Saffron, Grey, Sienna Brown.

The interior of the 1300 shared a common ambience with the 2000 range.

Only the subtle TC badges, fitted to the wings and boot lid, boasted of the second carburettor fitted to the TC model.

Honeysuckle and Ice Blue were added for 1973
ENGINE: 1493cc, four-cylinder, overhead valve, bore 73.7mm, stroke 87.5mm, power 61bhp, revised to 65bhp from late 1971.
GEARBOX: Four-speed with synchromesh on all forward speeds. Overall gearing ratios 1st 13.72:1, 2nd 8.73:1, 3rd 5.86:1, top 4.04:1, reverse 16.38:1.
FRONT-WHEEL DRIVE SYSTEM: Differential mounted below sump, drive shafts with flexible couplings. Differential ratio 4.55:1.
BRAKES: Hydraulic, operating front 8.75in diameter discs and rear drums 8in x 1.25in.
SUSPENSION: Front: independent with double wishbones and coil springs, telescopic dampers; rear: beam axle, radius arms, coil springs, telescopic dampers and anti-roll bar.

The profile appearance of the front-wheel drive 1500 was like its smaller-engined sibling, but the lengthened boot is apparent. The front adopted the twin headlight arrangement that would continue on the Dolomite in the future, and the interior styling was similar to the revised Mark 2 Triumph 2000. The deeply-dished hubcaps of the FWD cars are obvious.

STEERING: Rack and pinion.
DIMENSIONS: Length 162in (4115mm), width 61.75in (1569mm).
FUEL CAPACITY: 12.5 gallons (56.75 litres).
PRODUCTION: 66,353.
PERFORMANCE: Maximum speed 85mph and 0-60mph acceleration time of 17.1 seconds.

TRIUMPH TOLEDO

Toledo was a lower-cost version of 'AJAX' introduced in 1970, initially as a two-door saloon, with a four-door version added to the range in 1972. Unusually, the decision was taken by Triumph to revert to a conventional front engine and rear-drive layout. In March 1975, the two-door version was deleted from the model range.

Both two-door and four-door Toledo saloons were available.

COLOURS: At its introduction, the colour range for the Toledo was quite simple, and the following colours were available: White, Royal Blue, Wedgwood Blue, Sienna, Laurel Green, Damson, Signal Red, Valencia Blue, Saffron, Grey. In keeping with the fashion of the time for 1975 the following colours were available: Carmine Red, Pimento Red, White, Mimosa, Maple, Honeysuckle, British Racing Green, French Blue, Ice Blue, Delft Blue.
ENGINE: 1296cc, four-cylinder, overhead valve, bore 73.7mm, stroke 76mm, power 58bhp.

The rear of the Toledo continued to be similar to the 1300's ...

... while the front of the Toledo took on the styling of the 1500, but with single square headlamps.

GEARBOX: Four-speed with synchromesh on all forward speeds, remote floor change. Overall gearing ratios 1st 14.4:1, 2nd 8.86:1, 3rd 5.73:1, top 4.11:1, reverse 16.4:1.
REAR AXLE: Semi-floating. Ratio 4.11:1.
BRAKES: Hydraulic, operating 9in x 1.75in drums (front) and 8in x 1.5in drums (rear). From October 1972, front 8.75in diameter discs with servo assistance were added as standard equipment.
SUSPENSION: Front: independent with double wishbones and coil springs, telescopic dampers; rear: live axle, radius arms, coil springs and telescopic dampers.
STEERING: Rack and pinion.
DIMENSIONS: Length 156in (3962mm), width 61.75in (1569mm).
FUEL CAPACITY: 10.5 gallons (48 litres).
PRODUCTION: 119,182.
PERFORMANCE: The sales brochure gave figures for both two-door and four-door cars. Maximum speed for both was shown as 85mph, and 0-60mph acceleration was achieved in 18 seconds for the two-door with the four-door taking 0.5 seconds longer.

TRIUMPH 1500TC

In the same way that the 1300 became the Toledo, the 1500 became the 1500TC with a conversion to rear-wheel drive, and was first put on sale in 1973.

COLOURS: At its introduction, the following were available for the 1500TC: Carmine Red, Pimento Red, White, Maple, Honeysuckle, Emerald Green, Mallard, French Blue, Ice Blue, Sapphire Blue. For 1976, Mimosa was added, Delft Blue replaced Sapphire Blue, and British Racing Green replaced Emerald Green.
ENGINE: 1493cc, four-cylinder, overhead valve, bore 73.7mm, stroke 87.5mm, power 64bhp (DIN). Revisions in 1971 increased power to 71bhp (DIN).
GEARBOX: Four-speed with synchromesh on all forward speeds. Overall gearing ratios 1st 13.63:1, 2nd 8.39:1, 3rd 5.42:1, top 3.89:1, reverse 15.51:1.

The new 1500TC was given the Toledo-style frontal treatment, but retained the larger tail styling from the earlier 1500 model. (Image is of a Dolomite 1500, which, other than badging, is identical to 1500TC.)

Optional three-speed Borg-Warner automatic transmission. Overall gearing ratios 1st 9.31:1, 2nd 5.64:1, top 3.89:1, reverse 8.14:1.
REAR AXLE: Semi-floating. Ratio 3.89:1.
BRAKES: Hydraulic, with servo assistance operating front 8.75in diameter discs and rear drums 8in x 1.5in.
SUSPENSION: Front: independent with double wishbones and coil springs, telescopic dampers; rear: live axle, radius arms, coil springs and telescopic dampers.
STEERING: Rack and pinion.
DIMENSIONS: Length 162in (4115mm), width 61.75in (1569mm).
FUEL CAPACITY: 12.5 gallons (56.75 litres).
PRODUCTION: 25,549.
PERFORMANCE: Maximum speed 92mph and 0-60mph acceleration time of 14 seconds.

TRIUMPH DOLOMITE

Initially, the range-topping car in Triumph's medium-size range reintroduced a name used in the 1930s. Using the longer bodyshell of the 1500, 1972 saw the introduction of the car that was initially called the 'Dolomite' fitted with a new overhead cam engine. In due course, the Toledo became the Dolomite 1300, but now with the longer bodyshell, the 1500TC was renamed the Dolomite 1500 and the original Dolomite was then known as the Dolomite 1850. The ultimate Dolomite was the high-performance Dolomite Sprint, powered by a 16-valve single overhead camshaft; an ingenious innovation that was to win a Design Council Award for Triumph. In common with the then current practice, various levels of trim were offered, but even at the most basic, the Dolomite range was a very well appointed car.

With consolidation of the range, all engine capacities shared a common bodyshell with the longer tail. Lower specification models were fitted with single, rectangular headlamps, while further up the range, twin lamps were standard.

COLOURS: Dolomites were finished in a wide selection of the colours offered by Triumph. In the case of the Dolomite Sprint, a vinyl roof (a common accessory of the time) was fitted as standard. At introduction, the Dolomite was available in the following colours: Carmine, Pimento Red, White, Sienna, Honeysuckle, Emerald Green, Mallard, French Blue, Ice Blue, Sapphire Blue.

The introduction of the Dolomite Sprint brought some additional, exclusive colours: Mimosa and Magenta.

For 1977, the colour range had changed to White, Carmine Red, Flamenco Red, Inca Yellow, Russet Brown, Sandglow, Brooklands Green and Tahiti Blue.

ENGINE:
Dolomite 1300 – As Toledo.
Dolomite 1500 – As 1500TC.
Dolomite 1850 – 1854cc, four-cylinder,

Dating from 1977, this Dolomite 1300 interior is still opulent when compared to the car's competitors, but is beginning to bear some corporate similarity to other Leyland models of the same era. This interior will be very familiar to many people who learned to drive in one of the many such cars supplied to the British School of Motoring.

overhead cam, bore 87mm, stroke 78mm, power 91bhp (DIN).

Dolomite Sprint – 1998cc, four-cylinder, overhead cam, bore 90.3mm, stroke 78mm, power 127bhp (DIN).

GEARBOX:

Dolomite 1300 – As Toledo.

Dolomite 1500 – As 1500TC.

Dolomite 1850 – Four-speed with synchromesh on all forward speeds. Overall gearing ratios 1st 9.65:1, 2nd 6.47:1, 3rd 4.56:1, top 3.63:1, reverse 10.95:1. Optional overdrive on 3rd and top with 1:1.24 ratio.

Optional three-speed Borg-Warner automatic transmission. Overall gearing ratios 1st 7.82:1, 2nd 4.74:1, top 3.27:1, reverse 6.93:1.

Dolomite Sprint – Four-speed with synchromesh on all forward speeds. Overall gearing ratios 1st 10.31:1, 2nd 7.25:1, 3rd 4.80:1, top 3.45:1, reverse 11.62:1. Optional overdrive (until Spring 1975 and thereafter fitted as standard) on 3rd and top with 1:1.24 ratio.

Optional three-speed Borg-Warner automatic transmission. Overall gearing ratios 1st 8.25:1,

Topping the range is the high-performance Dolomite Sprint fitted with the award-winning 16-valve engine, and featuring alloy wheels and a vinyl roof as standard fittings.

The Dolomite 1500SE was a limited edition model fitted with walnut burr interior woodwork, cut pile carpets, and velour upholstery. Externally, vinyl coach lines were applied, along with unique badging. The wheels on this car have been replaced: originally Spitfire wheels were fitted.

2nd 5.00:1, top 3.45:1, reverse 6.93:1.
REAR AXLE: Dolomite 1300 and 1500 as Toledo and 1500TC. Dolomite 1850 and Dolomite Sprint semi-floating. Ratio 3.63:1 (Dolomite 1850) or 3.45:1 (Dolomite Sprint).
BRAKES: Hydraulic, with servo assistance operating front 8.75in diameter discs and rear drums 8in x 1.25in, 9in x 1.75in rear drum brakes (Dolomite Sprint).
SUSPENSION: Front: independent with double wishbones and coil springs, telescopic dampers; rear: live axle, radius arms, coil springs and telescopic dampers. Front and rear anti-roll bar on 1850 and Sprint.
STEERING: Rack and pinion.

DIMENSIONS: Length 162in (4115mm), width 61.75in (1569mm).
FUEL CAPACITY: 12.5 gallons (56.75 litres).
PRODUCTION: Dolomite 1300: 32,031, Dolomite 1500: 43,235, Dolomite 1850: 79,010 Dolomite Sprint: 22,941.
PERFORMANCE: In January 1972, *Motor* published a road test of an early Dolomite 1850, and recorded a maximum speed of 103.4mph and 0-60mph time of 11.3 seconds. A later test of a Dolomite Sprint published by *Autocar* in July 1973 recorded a maximum speed of 117mph and acceleration time of 8.7 seconds.

This is the interior of a Dolomite Sprint, finished in the same style as the larger 2500PI and 2500S saloons, and with a comprehensive range of instruments fitted as standard.

CHAPTER **12**

THE FINAL TRS

TR6

Retaining the mechanical elements of the TR5, Triumph subsequently produced the TR6, with revisions to the front and rear sections. Styling and tooling was produced by Karmann in Germany, and, despite the centre cockpit section of the car remaining broadly unaltered, the overall appearance was that of a new model. For the US market, the TR250 engine remained, but there was no unique model identifier. Very quickly, the TR6 gained the title of the 'Last of the Hairy Chested Sports Cars.' Introduced in 1968, the TR6 was to become the best selling of all TR models to date, with over 90% of production being exported.

A major revision for the 1973 model year was made, with revisions to the injection system, and a softer cam replaced the earlier part, reducing maximum power, but making the car easier to drive in traffic. At around the same time, the overdrive was revised with a different ratio, and now working only on the top two speeds. The earlier cars have the designations CP (injected) and CC (carburettor), with later cars identified as CR (injected) and CF.

COLOURS: At introduction, the following colours were available: Signal Red, Jasmine, Conifer Green, Royal Blue, Damson, White. Some cars were finished in Black to special order. Laurel Green, Sienna and Saffron were added during the life of the earlier CP/CC cars. For 1972, Pimento Red replaced Signal Red and Sapphire Blue replaced Royal Blue. During the production of the CR/CF cars the following colours were available for all or part of the time: Pimento Red, Carmine Red, Magenta, Sienna Brown, Maple Brown, Russet Brown, Mimosa, Inca (yellow), Topaz (orange), Emerald Green, British Racing Green, Java Green, Sapphire Blue, Mallard, French Blue, Delft Blue, Tahiti Blue, White.
ENGINE: Petrol injected model – 2498cc, six-cylinder, overhead valve, bore 74.7mm, stroke 95mm, petrol injected, power 150bhp

With the TR6, Triumph reverted to the traditional folding soft roof and optional, removable hardtop. The red car is fitted with original, factory-supplied wheels.

(gross), 142bhp (nett). With the change to the CR series, power 124bhp (DIN).
Carburettor model – 2498cc, six-cylinder, overhead valve, bore 74.7mm, stroke 95mm, twin carburettors, power 104bhp (DIN), rising to 106bhp (DIN).

Colour ranges changed regularly, but blue and red in various shades were always popular.

Whites and yellows also suited the style of the TR6.

GEARBOX: Petrol injected model – four-speed with synchromesh on all forward speeds, remote floor change. Overall gearing ratios: 1st 10.83:1, 2nd 6.94:1, 3rd 4.59:1, top 3.45:1, reverse 11.11:1.
Ratios revised during 1971 to give the following overall ratios: 1st 10.33:1, 2nd 7.25:1, 3rd 4.78:1, top 3.45:1, reverse 11.62:1. Optional overdrive on 2nd, 3rd and top with 1:1.22 ratio. During 1973, overdrive revised to operate on 3rd and top with 1:1.25 ratio.

Carburettor model – four-speed with synchromesh on all forward speeds, remote floor change. Overall gearing ratios: 1st 11.61:1, 2nd 7.43:1, 3rd 4.90:1, top 3.7:1, reverse 11.92:1
Ratios revised during 1971 to give the following overall ratios: 1st 11.06, 2nd 7.77:1, 3rd 5.14:1, top 3.7:1, reverse 12.47:1.
Optional overdrive as PI models.
REAR AXLE: Ratio 3.45:1 (injected models) 3.7:1 (carburettor models).
BRAKES: Hydraulic, operating front 10.9in diameter discs and rear drums 9in x 1.75in. Servo assistance fitted as standard.
SUSPENSION: Front: independent with coil springs and double wishbones, telescopic dampers, anti-roll bar; rear: independent using semi-trailing arms, coil springs and lever arm dampers.
STEERING: Rack and pinion.
DIMENSIONS: Length 155in (3937mm), width 58in (1473mm). US models were fitted with various low speed collision bumpers and over-riders, increasing the length in stages to 163.5in (4153mm).
FUEL CAPACITY: 11.25 gallons (51 litres).
PRODUCTION: 86,249.
PERFORMANCE: For the earlier PI cars, the sales brochure claimed a maximum speed of 125mph and 0-60mph time of 8.8 seconds, revising these figures to 116mph and 9.5 seconds for the later cars. For US cars fitted with twin carburettors, the equivalent figures were quoted as 111mph and 10.7 seconds

Various shades of green were available throughout the production of the TR6, with British Racing Green always popular. Magenta was only available for a short period, and surviving cars are now quite rare. This one has been modified to the owner's specific requirements.

rising to 11.5 seconds for the later cars. A road test by *Autocar* published in April 1969 indicated a maximum speed of 120mph and acceleration time to 60mph of 8.2 seconds.

The general layout of the instruments changed little from the first TR2 to the end of TR6 production. On later cars, the ignition key was repositioned onto the steering column, to meet requirements for an anti-theft lock.

TR6s sold outside of the USA received the petrol-injected 2.5-litre engine.

TR7 and TR8

Starting life as the Leyland Corporate sports car as a result of model rationalisation, the wedge-shaped car was styled by Harris Mann and was targeted, like previous TRs, at the US market. It was widely believed that changes to Federal regulations would outlaw open top cars, resulting in the car being designed as a coupé with a convertible following later, once the threat of restrictions receded. Power came from a 1998cc overhead cam engine for the TR7 and 3528cc V8 engine used in the TR8. The TR8 was only officially sold in the US. Built and marketed during a turbulent time in the British motor industry, TR7s were built first at Speke on Merseyside with production moving entirely to Canley before the final cars were built at Solihull. TR7 was only sold in the USA initially, with delivery commencing in 1975 and hindered by industrial action. Sales to other markets commenced around 18 months later. The convertible was launched in the US during 1979 and the rest of the world in 1980.

A more powerful version, TR8, was fitted with a V8 engine of the type fitted to the Rover 3500 of the period. An unfortunate combination of poor build quality, unfavourable currency exchange rates and a move in the US market to smaller engine cars did not help the success of the car with British Leyland losing money on every car that was sold. Although never formally marketed outside of the US, a very small

TR7s were initially only available as fixed head coupés. Bright colours suited the car well.

A full-length sunroof, as fitted here, gives many of the benefits of an open car.

number of UK market cars were built and have survived. In addition to the V8 version, a small number of cars were fitted with the 16-valve Dolomite Sprint engine and badged as TR7 Sprint, but the project was cancelled.

With the final car being built in 1981, the TR7 and TR8 were the very last home designed cars to wear the Triumph badge.

COLOURS: Over a long production build at three different plants, the colour range of the TR7/TR8 was complicated. The following collates the colours available from each assembly plant. Not all colours were available for the entire production period and not all were officially available on both coupés and convertibles.

Speke built cars – White, French Blue, Delft Blue, Tahiti Blue, Pimento Red, Carmine Red, Flamenco Red, British Racing Green, Tara Green*, Java Green, Mimosa, Topaz, Inca Yellow, Maple, Russet.

Canley built cars – White, Inca Yellow, Tumeric Yellow, Vermillion Red, Carmine Red, Carnelian Red, Richelieu Red, Russet Brown, Pageant Blue, Persian Aqua*, Brooklands Green,

The chiselled front required pop up headlamps to be fitted.

Bold colours and patterns were chosen for the upholstery.

Once it became clear that the threat of open cars being outlawed in the US had ended, a TR7 convertible quickly appeared.

Both coupé and convertible cars are genuine TR8s, the convertible being a right-hand drive development vehicle.

Poseidon Green*, Triton Green*, Silver*, Midas Gold*.
Solihull built cars – White, Midas Gold*, Pharaoh Gold*, Beige, Poseidon Green*, Triton Green*, Carnelian Red, Bordeaux Red*,

Cavalry Blue, Persian Aqua*, Cashmere Gold*, Silver*.
* *Colours shown with an asterisk are metallic paint finishes.*
ENGINE:
TR7 – 1998cc, four-cylinder, overhead cam, bore 90.3mm, stroke 78mm, power 105bhp (DIN) for non USA model; 92bhp (DIN) for US models.
TR8 – 3528cc, eight-cylinder, overhead valve, bore 88.9mm, stroke 71.1mm, power 133bhp(DIN) except cars sold in California fitted with Lucas fuel-injection, 137bhp (DIN).
GEARBOX:
TR7 – four-speed with synchromesh on all forward speeds, remote floor change. Overall gearing ratios: 1st 9.65:1, 2nd 6.47:1, 3rd 4.56:1, top 3.63:1, reverse 10.95:1. Five-speed with synchromesh on all forward speeds, remote floor change, fitted to later models. Overall gearing ratios: 1st 12.95:1, 2nd 8.14:1, 3rd 5.44:1, 4th 3.9:1, top 3.25:1, reverse 13.37:1.
Optional Borg-Warner model 65 epicyclic automatic. Overall gearing ratios 1st 7.82:1, 2nd 4.74:1, top 3.27:1, reverse 6.83:1.
TR8 – five-speed with synchromesh on all forward speeds, remote floor change. Overall gearing ratios: 1st 10.23:1, 2nd 6.44:1, 3rd 4.31:1, 4th 3.08:1, top 2.56:1, reverse 10.56:1.

Optional Borg-Warner model 65 epicyclic automatic. Overall gearing ratios: 1st 7.36:1, 2nd 4.47:1, top 3.08:1, reverse 6.44:1.
REAR AXLE: Live rear axle. Ratio 3.63:1 (four-speed transmission), 3.9:1 (five-speed transmission), 3.27:1 (automatic), 3:08:1 (TR8).
BRAKES: Hydraulic, operating front 9.7in diameter discs and rear drums 8in x 1.5in, except with five-speed gearbox or TR8, then 9in x 1.75in rear drums. Servo assistance fitted as standard.
SUSPENSION: Front: independent with coil springs and MacPherson struts, anti-roll bar; rear: live axle, coil springs radius arms telescopic dampers and anti-roll bar.
STEERING: Rack and pinion, power assisted on TR8.
DIMENSIONS: Length 160in (4064mm), width 66.25in (1683mm). US models were fitted with different bumpers, giving overall length of 165.4in (4201mm).
FUEL CAPACITY: 12 gallons (55 litres).

This is a genuine TR7 Sprint, sold off by the factory.

PRODUCTION: TR7 – 112,368; **TR8** – 2722.
PERFORMANCE: The brochures were very light on performance data; contemporary reports give a maximum speed of 108mph and 0-60mph time of 10.8 seconds for a UK specification, Speke built car. For a TR8, figures show a maximum speed of 135mph and 0-60mph time of 7.7 seconds.

Model badging changed with each factory move. Speke-built cars wore the TR7 outline vinyl, Canley-built cars were given a Triumph laurel, and Solihull cars were fitted with a smaller laurel badge. TR8 models were fitted with a text vinyl.

CHAPTER 13

TRIUMPH STAG

The car that many considered to be Triumph's answer to the Mercedes-Benz SL began as a styling exercise by Michelotti, who was looking to create a GT car based on the Triumph 2000 to use as an advertisement for his skills. A spare prototype 2000 was unofficially loaned, and in early 1966, the resulting car was shown to Harry Webster, Triumph's Director of Engineering, when the decision was taken to utilise the design for a new model. But first, the characteristics of the new style would be used to update the existing 2000 range to create the Mark Two model. Despite the visual similarities, none of the body panels used on the two cars are interchangeable.

First put on sale in 1970, the Stag is a rare example where the development code name finally became the product name. Motive power came from Triumph's own three-litre V8 engine, and transmission was either via a three-speed Borg-Warner automatic or a four-speed with optional overdrive manual gearbox. Unfortunately,

Convertible roof up or down, or with the hardtop fitted, Triumph's Stag is a stylish car.

the Stag quickly gained a not entirely undeserved reputation for poor reliability. Overheating was frequently a problem and

timing chain stretch or breakage could result in terminal engine damage. Despite the US being the primary target market, the poor reputation of the car resulted in it being withdrawn from sale after just three years.

During the production life of the car, there were few significant changes. Later cars can be recognised by a coach stripe and stainless steel sill cover. Officially, the cars were built in four individual factory 'sanctions,' but are frequently referred to as 'Mark One' and 'Mark Two' cars, with some overlap.

COLOURS: Colour options changed regularly and hardtops were always supplied in body colour. At the introduction, customers could choose from the following: White, Damson, Signal Red, Laurel Green, Royal Blue, Saffron. For 1972, Royal Blue was deleted and Sienna Brown added. For 1973, Signal Red was replaced with Carmine Red and Pimento Red was added, along with three blue colours: French, Sapphire and Mallard. Mimosa replaced Saffron. For 1974, Magenta was added and Maple replaced Sienna Brown.

There were minor changes reflecting fashion until 1977 when the following full range was available: White, Carmine Red, Pimento Red, Maple Brown, Russet Brown, French Blue, Delft Blue, Pageant Blue, Tahiti Blue, Inca Yellow, Mimosa Yellow, Java Green, Topaz Orange.

ENGINE: 2997cc, eight cylinders in V formation, overhead cam (single cam per bank), bore 86mm, stroke 64.5mm, power 145bhp (DIN). USA models 127bhp (DIN).

GEARBOX: Four-speed with synchromesh on all forward speeds, remote floor change. Overall gearing ratios 1st 11.08:1, 2nd 7.77:1, 3rd 5.13:1, top 3.7:1, reverse 13.81:1.

Optional overdrive on 3rd and top with 1:1.22 ratio (until 1973), 1:1.26 ratio (from 1973). Overdrive fitted as standard from late 1972. Optional three-speed automatic (Borg Warner model 35 on early cars, model 65 on later)

Multiple shades of green were available during the production run.

Blue also suited the car well.

Signal, Pimento and Carmine Red were also available.

with torque converter and floor mounted shift Overall gearing ratios 1st 8.84:1, 2nd 5.37:1, top 3.7:1, reverse 7.73:1.

REAR AXLE: Differential mounted to rear subframe, sliding joint drive shafts. Ratio 3.7:1.

BRAKES: Hydraulic dual circuit, operating front 10.6in diameter discs and rear drums 9in x 2.25in. Servo assisted.

SUSPENSION: Front: independent with MacPherson strut and coil spring, telescopic dampers; rear: independent using semi-trailing arms, coil springs and telescopic dampers.

STEERING: Rack and pinion, power assisted.

DIMENSIONS: Length 173.75in (4413mm), width 63.5in (1613mm).

FUEL CAPACITY: 14 gallons (63.6 litres).

PRODUCTION: 25,877.

PERFORMANCE: The sales brochure boasted a maximum speed of 118mph and acceleration from rest to 60mph in 9.5 seconds. *Motor* published a road test in September 1970 in which they achieved 125mph on the straight of the MIRA test track, and predicted a maximum speed of 130mph in perfect conditions. Their acceleration test matched the factory figures.

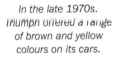

In the late 1970s. Triumph offered a range of brown and yellow colours on its cars.

Chapter 14

TRIUMPH ACCLAIM

In the late 1970s, British Leyland urgently needed to replace the Dolomite which, in its various forms since its introduction as the 1300, had then been in production for some ten years. The existing volume cars, although selling in reasonable numbers, were outclassed in the market, and the replacements which would be sold as Metro, Maestro and Montego were many years away. The company investigated a partnership, with both Renault and Chrysler's European operations being considered as possible partners. At the time, Japanese imports were selling well in all European countries, and causing concern with the indigenous manufacturers, resulting in Japanese imports being restricted to a voluntary limit of 11% of the market.

It therefore suited both partners when BL and Honda agreed to build and sell the new model Honda Ballade as a BL model, badged as a Triumph. Assembled in the UK, and containing some local content, with an interior revised to suit European taste, and the suspension re-profiled to meet local conditions, this car became the first Japanese model to be assembled in Europe. The four-cylinder overhead cam engine was a Honda unit, and power to the front wheels was delivered either through a standard five-speed manual gearbox or the 'Hondamatic' automatic three-speed system marketed as 'Trio-matic.'

Despite initial intentions to build the car at Triumph's Canley plant, the body was eventually assembled at the former Pressed Steel plant in Cowley, Oxford, and transported by covered conveyor across the Oxford Ring Road to the final assembly plant on the site of the old Morris Motors. Deliveries commenced in 1981. Build quality surpassed anything previously emerging from British Leyland and the car was notable for the low level of warranty claims. It was finished to a high standard and offered initially in three trim levels (HL, HLS and CD) with an entry level 'L' trim being added as production came to an end in 1984. The

A popular choice for the biennial 'Round Britain Reliability Run' charity event organised by Club Triumph, these Acclaims prove their reliability by completing a 2000 mile journey in 48 hours. Although every other Triumph model in the event is older than these cars, most of the Acclaims are unrestored, and are often purchased from the small ads just for this event, which they complete with little prior preparation.

specialist coachwork business of Ladbroke Avon produced a factory-approved rework of the car, marketed as Avon Acclaim. This added a two-tone paint finish, vinyl roof, additional rubbing strips, and a leather trimmed interior. A performance upgrade featuring a turbocharger was also available.

Whether the car is considered as a true Triumph or not is a question still not settled. But the car was important in forging the strategic partnership between BL (and, in due course, Austin-Rover) and Honda, resulting in an attractive and commercially successful range of cars sold under the revamped Rover brand. Manufacturing statistics show that the only Triumph-badged model to sell more than the Acclaim was the Herald 1200, and that was over a significantly longer production period.

COLOURS: The following were available on all trim levels: White, Rattan Beige, Monza Red, Clove Brown, Eclipse Blue. Available on HLS and CD models and as an option at extra cost on L and HL models were the following: Black, Silver Leaf*, Cashmere Gold*, Oporto Red*, Opaline Green*, Zircon Blue*.
*Colours marked with an asterisk are metallic finishes.
ENGINE: 1335cc, four cylinders, overhead cam, bore 72mm, stroke 82mm, power 70bhp (DIN).
GEARBOX: Four-speed with synchromesh on all forward speeds, remote floor change. Overall gearing ratios 1st 13.54:1, 2nd 8.19:1, 3rd 5.48:1, 4th 3.93:1, top 3.31:1, reverse 13.54:1.
Optional three-speed automatic with torque converter and floor mounted shift.
Overall gearing ratios 1st 6.36:1, 2nd 4.25:1, top 3.20:1, reverse 7.73:1.
FRONT-WHEEL DRIVE SYSTEM: Unequal length drive shafts, constant velocity joints. Ratio 4.64:1 (automatic 3.11:1).
BRAKES: Hydraulic dual circuit, operating front 8.5in diameter discs and rear drums 7.1in x 1in. Servo assisted.
SUSPENSION: front: independent with MacPherson strut, coil spring, anti-roll bar; rear: independent with MacPherson strut, coil spring and trailing arm location.
STEERING: Rack and pinion.
DIMENSIONS: Length 161in (4089mm), width 63in (1600mm).
FUEL CAPACITY: 10 gallons (46.4 litres).

Two examples of Acclaims that, despite being over 30 years old, still look as though they are fresh from the dealer. The colours are typical of the mid-1980s.

PRODUCTION: 133,626.
PERFORMANCE: The marketing brochures were silent on all aspects of performance, concentrating instead on fuel economy. *Autocar* published a road test report in October 1981 and reported a maximum speed of 92mph (in 4th gear) and acceleration to 60mph in 12.9 seconds.

Early Vanguard pickups had a rounded tail and lower height load area.

With its powerful and high-torque engine, this Vanguard has been converted into a useful breakdown recovery vehicle.

CHAPTER 15

STANDARD AND TRIUMPH COMMERCIAL VEHICLES

Commercial vehicles were a small part of the business for Standard-Triumph and, with one exception, the Standard Atlas, were all derived from the car models of the period. Commercial versions commenced with the Phase I Vanguard.

Vanguard commercials

All commercial models of the early Vanguard were based on the Phase I and Phase IA. A pickup was built with early models having a rounded load area, later models being more square. The Royal Air Force was an important customer for the pickup, with production continuing until 1958 when it was replaced with the Phase III model.

Pick-up trucks were always popular in Australia and New Zealand, where they are known as 'utes' (an abbreviation of utility vehicle), and were built locally by Standard's Australian subsidiary. Phase III utes are far more common than the UK-built pickup.

A twelve-hundredweight panel van was

Later pickups used a larger load-carrying space.

displayed at the Commercial Motor Show in 1948. The body shell of the panel van and estate car were broadly similar with the panel van having only two doors. Massey Ferguson were loyal customers for this vehicle.

Commercial vehicles were usually supplied from the factory with limited brightwork, and finished in primer as it would be usual for a new vehicle to be finished and sign written for the customer's exact requirements.

Three ambulance conversions were also built. Although the front of the vehicle had the appearance of a Vanguard, it was constructed on the modified chassis of a Renown.

Standard 10 based commercials

Two Standard 10 based commercials were introduced in 1954; a 6-cwt panel van with a capacity of 90 cubic feet and a pickup. The van had the usual twin opening rear doors, and the pickup was fitted with a tipper style drop tailboard and the provision for a canvas cover to be fitted. In both models, the cab area was fitted with winding windows and opening quarter light vents. The styling of the van was like the familiar Morris Minor van with the load area being raised above the cab area. In the UK, two models were marketed by conversion specialists Martin Walter, better known by their trademark of 'Dormobile.' The Standard 10/Martin Walter Dormobile took as its basis a 10 van, and added windows to the rear van area. A rear seat was added and fitted so that it could

A Phase III Vanguard pickup. This example has badges to indicate it is fitted with a six-cylinder engine.

A Vanguard-based panel van was also available.

The Standard 10 made a popular light van, and was once a regular sight on the roads.

A pickup was also available in the Standard 10 model range. This example has been fitted with a canvas 'tilt' cover and frame.

With most having had a very hard-working life, very few Atlas vans have survived. This is a nicely restored example, finished in the blue shade used by the Triumph works rally team.

form a double bed, or be folded against the front seats to provide a large load area. The 'Utilecon' was similar, but only provided the folding rear seat to increase the load area. Both models were said to appeal to business users who needed a van during the working week and a family car for the weekend.

Standard Atlas

Atlas was designed specifically as a commercial vehicle, delivered as a panel van or as a pickup, and with the option of forward hinged or sliding doors. Panels vans were converted to minibuses and small motor caravans, or as they were frequently called at the time 'caravanettes.' Introduced in 1958, the market was already well served with products from BMC and especially Bedford, whose CA van was as ubiquitous as the Ford Transit was to become, following its introduction in 1965. Standard's key advantage with the Atlas was its very tight turning circle, partly achieved by a very narrow track, and good visibility, making it an ideal vehicle for town centre deliveries. It was rated as a 10cwt or 12cwt payload, depending on whether a passenger was to be carried, but surprisingly, for a vehicle of its size, was powered by a 948cc engine as used in the Standard 10, slightly detuned to allow the van to run on commercial grade fuel available at the time. The engine was placed centrally between the front seats, which were themselves placed directly over the front wheels, giving the advantage of a flat cab floor. At the rear on the panel van, a large one-piece door was hinged on the offside.

Addressing comments regarding the lack of power, in 1960 a new model Atlas Major was introduced, using the 1670cc, as fitted to the Standard Ensign, and a remote gear change was now fitted. Following the acquisition of Standard-Triumph by Leyland Motors, the Atlas was rebranded as the Leyland 15 or Leyland 20, reflecting the payload in hundredweight, and power was now from the 2138cc engine, as fitted in the TR4, but suitably detuned. A diesel engine was also available of the type used in the

Phase II Vanguard and Ferguson tractor. Production continued until 1968.

Specification for original Atlas:
COLOURS: Usually supplied from the factory finished in primer.
ENGINE: 948cc, four-cylinder, overhead valve, bore 63mm, stroke 76mm, power 30.5bhp.
GEARBOX: Four-speed with synchromesh on top three speeds, change lever mounted at rear of seats. Overall gearing ratios 1st 28.44:1, 2nd 16.38:1, 3rd 5.48:1, 4th 9.68:1, top 6.66:1, reverse 28.44:1.
REAR AXLE: Fully floating, final drive ratio 6.66:1.
BRAKES: Hydraulic drums front and back. Front 9 x 1.75; rear 8 x 1.25.
SUSPENSION: Front: independent with transverse leaf spring, telescopic dampers; rear semi elliptic springs with lever type dampers.
STEERING: Recirculating ball.
DIMENSIONS: Length 161in (4089mm), width 67in (1702mm).
FUEL CAPACITY: 10 gallons (46.4 litres).
PERFORMANCE: *Commercial Motor* undertook a comprehensive test and reported a time of 28.6 seconds to reach 40mph. A cruising speed of 40mph to 45mph was mentioned and a maximum speed of 50mph.

Triumph Courier

Introduced in February 1962, Triumph's first and only van met with much approval from specialist magazine *Commercial Motor*, who thought it was 'probably the most luxurious commercial vehicle ever made.' With a nominal load rating of 5cwt, the van was marketed to small businesses and was unusual for small commercial vehicles of the time, in that a passenger seat was fitted as standard. Mechanically identical to the Triumph Herald 1200 estate, the only differences were a simplified dashboard and a plywood floor in the rear compartment.

Front and rear images of Triumph's Courier small van. Like the Atlas pictured, the blue Courier is finished in the style of a Works rally team support vehicle, while the white van is a promotional vehicle for one of the Triumph owners' clubs.

APPENDIX A

STANDARD-TRIUMPH AS AN INDUSTRY SUPPLIER

Throughout the 1930s, the Standard Motor Company had built up a profitable side business supplying major components and sub-assemblies to other vehicle manufacturers. SS-Cars, the forerunner to Jaguar, was a major customer for Standard engines and transmissions. Triumph, conversely, used bought-in items, taking engines for some of its products from Coventry-Climax. With the merger of the two businesses and the decline of the smaller independent manufacturers, opportunities to supply components and sub-assemblies outside of the Standard-Triumph product range declined but did not disappear entirely. In particular, the early TR chassis, engines and transmissions found use elsewhere in the motor industry, as did the chassis and running gear of the Herald. Below are some examples of other manufacturers who found Triumph to be a valuable supplier.

A side view of the Swallow Doretti shows the attractive styling of the car, which was markedly different to that of the TR2.

Inside the cockpit, there some similarities to the TR2 in the controls and gauges that reveal the Triumph origins of the Doretti. The positioning of the instruments simplified conversion between left- and right-hand drive.

Swallow Doretti

At the same time as SS-Cars evolved into Jaguar, the original motorcycle sidecar business of Swallow was sold, and came under the control of specialist steel components manufacturer, Tube Investments. Following a meeting between a director of Tube Investments and a US business partner, who both had ambitions to enter the booming sports car market, a plan was devised to fulfil this wish, which resulted in the Swallow Doretti. The entire drivetrain of the engine gearbox and rear axle was sourced from Standard-Triumph and was identical to that used in the TR2, but the chassis was a tubular style of similar design to the TR2 but longer and wider. Alloy bodywork was constructed over steel tubs mounted to the chassis. The overall result was a stylish car that combined the front styling of a contemporary Ferrari and the rear of the Austin-Healey 100. The name was donated by the daughter of the Californian distributor, Dorothy Deen who modified her name to Doretti to give it an Italian feel. Finished to a high standard, the car sold well, until pressure on Tube Investments from other motor industry customers who were concerned that the success of the Doretti in the market was affecting their own sales opportunities brought production to a premature end.

Visitors to this major classic car exhibition found it difficult to believe that, underneath the stylish and obviously Italian design from the turn of the 1960s, could be found the simple mechanicals of a Triumph TR3.

Triumph Italia

At first glance, this car may be mistaken for a Ferrari or Maserati. Its origin lies with the Italian distributor for Standard-Triumph who wanted to market a stylish Italian coupé built on the simple and rugged mechanicals of a Triumph TR3. The car was styled by Michelotti, and handmade coachwork was fitted to the completed chassis at the Vignale facility in Turin. Although mechanically simple, the bespoke bodywork and potential costs of restoration resulted in the cars going into a decline until recent years, when they have achieved a greater recognition.

Bond Equipe

In the second half of the 1950s, a new market for micro-cars emerged, fuelled by a shortage of traditional cars and the desire of motorcycle riders for more comfort. These micro-cars sometimes took the form of traditional cars reduced in size and powered by motorcycle engines. Three-wheelers were common as these vehicles were covered by a motorcycle licence. Two firms emerged that would be successful in marketing small, three-wheel cars: Reliant and Bond. The market for these declined in the early 1960s, leading the Bond company to consider a move into more conventional cars. Without the facilities to build from scratch, Bond chose to adapt an existing design to his requirements; the Herald, built on a conventional chassis was a perfect platform. A design for a GT 2+2 car was presented to Standard-Triumph, and was considered to be complementary to its product range. An agreement was reached for Bond to be supplied with the chassis, bulkhead, windscreen, floor and doors, to which a fibreglass body was fitted. Power and transmission originally came from a Spitfire 1147cc engine and gearbox, later enlarged to a 1296cc engine. In 1967, Bond revised the Equipe to use the mechanical components of the Vitesse, and introduced a convertible version. Production ended in 1970 after the sale of Bond to Reliant.

TVR2500M

TVR introduced its 'M' series in 1972 following the earlier Vixen models. The overall styling of the car, built from glass fibre was continued, and three models were available, determined

Viewed from the side, some similarities between the Italia and Michelotti's eventual TR4 design for Triumph can be seen.

A late model Bond Equipe built on Vitesse running gear. The resemblance to the Vitesse and Herald is clear, while the bonnet air scoop, headlamp surrounds, and wheel trims were all sourced from Triumph's 2000 saloon.

This TVR 2500M shares many of its mechanical components with the TR250 and US version of the TR6 from the same era, but the fibreglass coupé bodywork provides an entirely different driving experience.

by the engine fitted. Two models, the 1600M and 3000M were powered with engines supplied by Ford, but between these two sat the 2500M that utilised the same 2.5-litre, six-cylinder engine, as fitted to the TR250 and US versions of the TR6 with a key advantage that it had already met the US Federal emission requirements. In addition to the engine, the front suspension, steering, gearbox and differential were all provided by Triumph, being sourced from the TR6.

Appendix B

COMMISSION NUMBERS

Prior to the adoption of internationally standardised VIN numbering, Standard-Triumph used a logical series of alphanumeric combinations to uniquely identify each car produced, referred to as the vehicles 'Commission' number. The commission number followed the following general format:

The first character may be a number, indicating that the car was assembled overseas from a kit of 'Completely Knocked Down' parts. For cars assembled at a UK factory, this character will not be present.

A series of one, two or three alphabet characters indicates the model range, as shown in the table below. In the case of later Triumph cars, if the first letter is A, the car was built at Speke, otherwise it was built at Canley. This is always present, and is followed by a string of digits that identifies the actual car. The numbers are contiguous in groups, but did not start at 1, and simply increment up to the final car to be built.

Standard-Triumph model range designator

18TD	1800 Town and Country Saloon	FD	Spitfire Mark 3
18TR	Roadster, 1.8-litre engine	FDU	Spitfire Mark 3 (USA)
20TR	Roadster, 2-litre engine	FH	Spitfire Mark IV
ACG	TR7 (UK/Europe)	FK	Spitfire Mark IV (USA)
ACH	TR7 Sprint	FL	Spitfire Mark IV (Sweden)
ACL	TR7 (USA)	FM	Spitfire 1500
ACN	TR7 V8	G	Herald 948 and S
ACT	TR7 convertible	GA	Herald 1200
ACW	TR7 (USA)	GB	Herald 1200 (export)
ADF	Toledo four-door	GD	Herald 12/50
ADG	Toledo	GE	Herald 13/60
ADH	Toledo two-door	GY	Herald 948 TC
ADM	Toledo (1500 engine)	HB	Vitesse 6
ADP	Toledo four-door (1500 engine)	HC	Vitesse 2 litre
ADS	Toledo four-door (1500 engine)	KC	GT6 MK1 and MK2
ADV	Toledo	KE	GT6 MK3
ADW	Toledo (1500 engine)	KF	GT6 MK3 (USA)
BE	Standard 10	KG	GT6 MK3 (Sweden)
CC	TR6 USA (early)	LD	Stag
CD	TR250	LE	Stag
CF	TR6 USA (late)	MB	2000 MK1
CP	TR5, TR6 PI (early)	MD	2.5PI MK1
CR	TR6 PI (late)	ME	2000 MK2
CS	Standard Eight	MG	2.5PI MK2
CT	TR4 and live axle 4A	ML	2000TC
CTC	TR4A IRS	MM	2500TC
DEC	Vanguard Phase II Diesel	MP	2500S
DF	Toledo four-door	PN	Standard Pennant
DH	Toledo two-door	RD	1300 FWD
EL	Ensign deluxe	RF	1300 TC
EN	Ensign	TBE	Triumph 10 (Standard 10 for USA market)
FC	Spitfire 4 and Mark 2		

continues overleaf

TCF	TR3B	TS	TR2/TR3/TR3A
TCG	TR7 (UK/Europe)	TSF	TR3B
TCN	TR8 coupé	TT	Mayflower
TCT	TR7 convertible (USA)	VA	Dolomite Sprint
TCV	TR8 convertible	VA	Vanguard
TCV	TR7 coupé (USA)	W	Vanguard Six
TCW	TR7 (USA)	WB	1500 FWD
TDA	Renown	WE	Dolomite 1850HL
TDA	2000 Town and Country Saloon	WF	Dolomite 1850
TDB	Renown	WG	Dolomite 1300 & 1500
TDB	Renown	WK	Dolomite 1500HL
TDC	Renown	Y	Herald 948 coupé or convertible
TDD	Vanguard Sportsman	YC	1500 TC

A series of alphabetic characters will then follow. In many cases, the first two characters will be 'DL,' and any further letters will indicate body style or options, examples being the following:

DL	Common across saloon models
CV	Convertible (especially Herald and Vitesse)
CP	Coupé (especially Herald)
RS	Factory fitted sunshine roof (Herald 12/50, for example)
PU	Pick up (commercial vehicle)
L	Signifies left-hand drive
SC or SW	Estate car
V	Van (commercial vehicle)
O	Overdrive
BW, BG or A	Automatic

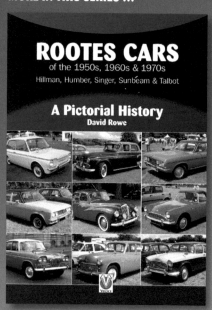
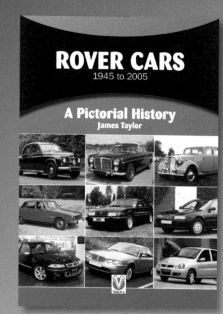
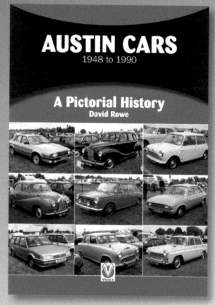
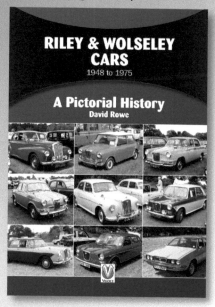

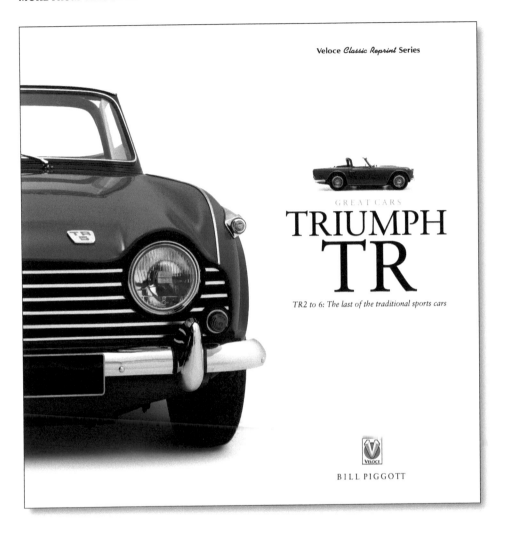

Veloce *Classic Reprint* Series

GREAT CARS

TRIUMPH TR

TR2 to 6: The last of the traditional sports cars

BILL PIGGOTT

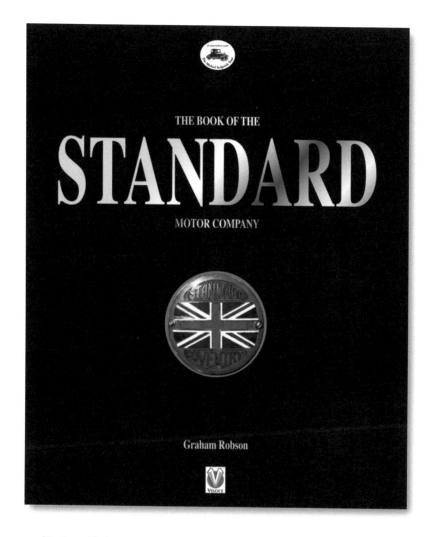

THE BOOK OF THE

STANDARD

MOTOR COMPANY

Graham Robson

Starting with the original Standard prototype of 1903, this book covers the scores of Standard models built until the brand was discontinued in 1963 (Britain) and 1987 (India). It also covers the Ferguson tractor involvement, military aero-engine manufacture, military aircraft manufacturer (including Beaufighter and Mosquito fighter-bombers), Rolls-Royce Avon turbo-jet military engine manufacture, and Triumph cars.

ISBN: 978-1-845843-43-4
Hardback • 25x20.7cm • 208 pages • 262 colour and b&w pictures

For more information and price details, visit our website at www.veloce.co.uk
email: info@veloce.co.uk • Tel: +44(0)1305 260068

ESSENTIAL BUYER'S GUIDES ...

ISBN: 978-1-787112-72-8
Paperback • 19.5x13.9cm
64 pages • 95 pictures

ISBN: 978-1-787112-85-8
Paperback • 19.5x13.9cm
64 pages • 95 pictures

ISBN: 978-1-845840-26-6
Paperback • 19.5x13.9cm
64 pages • 101 colour pictures

ISBN: 978-1-845843-16-8
Paperback • 19.5x13.9cm
64 pages • 108 colour pictures

ISBN: 978-1-787112-80-3
Paperback • 19.5x13.9cm
64 pages • 102 colour pictures

Thinking of buying a classic Triumph?

Having one of these books in your pocket is just like having a real marque expert by your side.
Benefit from the author's years of Triumph experience, learn how to spot a bad car quickly and
how to assess a promising one like a professional. Get the right car at the right price!

See more in this series on the Veloce website – over 100 titles available

For more information and price details, visit our website at www.veloce.co.uk
email: info@veloce.co.uk • Tel: +44(0)1305 260068

INDEX